THE SAMARITAN CHRONICLE

or the Book of Joshua, the son of Nun

Translated from the Arabic, with notes by:

Oliver Turnbull Crane (1890)

Edited by:

D.P. Curtin

Dalcassian
Publishing
Company

PHILADELPHIA, PA

THE SAMARITAN CHRONICLE

Library of Congress Cataloging-in-Publication Data

Charité du Samaritain.   59

Preface

The Samaritan Book of Joshua was first brought to the notice of European scholars by the eminent Orientalist, Joseph J. Scaliger, who obtained a manuscript of it from the Samaritans of Cairo, in the year 1584. This MS. was deposited by him in the library of the University of Leyden, and for a long period remained the only copy of the work in Europe; in fact, it is only within the last half of the present century that other MSS. have been obtained; one of these is now in the possession of the British Museum, and another is said to be in the library of trinity College, Cambridge. To the celebrated Swiss theologian and scholar, Johann Heinrich Hottinger, is due the credit of making the contents of this work fully known to scholars; this he did in his Exercitationes Anti-Moriniance de Pentateucho Samaritano, published in 1644, wherein he gave a condensed Latin translation, or rather epitome, of the whole chronicle: he likewise treated of it in other of his writings, especially in his Smegma Orient, (1657), which contains a fair resume' of its contents. Hottinger's works remained the principle source from which scholars drew their information of the character and contents of this chronicle of the Samaritans, until in the year 1848, T.W.J. Juynboll edited the Arabic text of the Leyden MS. with a complete Latin translation to which were added elaborate dissertations and copious critical notes. This translation of Juynboll's at once superseded all that had preceded it, and has ever since remained the standard.

The translation now offered- the first that has ever been attempted in English- is made directly from the Arabic text as printed by Juynboll, while the MS. in the British Museum has been examined and consulted in many cases. To those who may take the trouble to compare this English translation with Juynboll's Latin, it may occasion surprise to find that, in the interpretation of a considerable number of passages they materially differ; if such will, however, only turn to the original Arabic and consult it, the writer confidently believes that the English rendering will be found to more exactly represent the original than the Latin. It should be borne in mind, however, that the Leyden MS. is in the Samaritan characters, though written in the Arabic language, which the scribe often wrote in a most careless and negligent manner, and hence the MS. is in many places exceedingly difficult to decipher. Juynboll edited it in Arabic characters, but, on account of the wretchedness of the writing, was often driven to conjectural readings and emendations, yet he always placed in the margin the exact, or supposed, words of the text, thus affording the student an opportunity to form an independent judgment as to the justice and accuracy of his emendations, and upon careful consideration one is sometimes forced to the conclusion that Juynboll has unintentionally erred, both in his reading of the text and in his conjectural corrections, and that the discarded words in the margin are in some cases to be preferred to his attempted improvements. These facts will explain some of the variations which distinguish this translation from the Latin one of Juynboll.

It is not the intention of the writer to detract one whit from the praise which is due to Juynboll, for the care he bestowed upon his work and for his truly able translation and the scholarly and erudite notes that he added to it; to all of which the writer here makes acknowledgment of his great indebtedness.

Next to the Jews there is scarcely any people that excite the interest of biblical students more warmly than the Samaritans. Their origin, their history, their literature and their traditions are questions that have brought to their investigation a succession of able scholars, and are to day still subjects of intense interest and research. The present translation is put forth with the hope that it may not be unwelcome to the many who are interested in these subjects, but to whom this Chronicle in the original language has been a sealed book.

Among the Samaritans themselves this book is not held to be of Divine inspiration- for they believe that only the five books of Moses are inspired- nevertheless, they greatly revere it and hold it in the highest estimation, and believe it to contain a true and authentic history of the period of which it treats. As to when it was composed and who was its author we have no positive knowledge. From the inscription which the Leyden MS.

bears we learn that the first part of the codex, as it now stands, was written in A.D. 1362-3, and the latter part in A.D. 1513. Juynboll's researches led him to the conclusion that it was redacted into its present form about A.D. 1300, out of earlier documents. This is probably the fact, and it is all that can be safely predicated as to the time of its compilation.

A marked feature of the book is the number of legends and traditions it contains, some of which- so far as we are aware- are to be met with nowhere else. Most of them, however, are intimately connected with similar legends current in the East, and show a common origin with those of the Jews, and frequently with those of the Mohammedans. In the notes an effort has been made to notice such Jewish or Moslem legends and traditions as are identical or show an affinity with those mentioned in the text, in order that the reader may see wherein the various versions agree or differ. Care has been taken also to identify, so far as it was possible, all places or localities mentioned in the Chronicle, and to give their ancient Hebrew names. This, it is believed, will not be without value to all such as are unfamiliar with the modern Arabic names of the places in Palestine, and who might otherwise be at a loss to know the Arabic names in the Chronicle.

To all who are interested in the history, geography and legends of Palestine this Chronicle of the Samaritans will be of particular interest; and while it is not to be denied that many of its statements are incredible, still the fact that much of it contains is of true value and is not to be ignored, but may be used discriminately to good advantage by scholars to shed light upon a large range of subjects, our knowledge of which is and always has been extremely limited; in support of this we might refer to the recognition it has received at the hands of such writers as Bishop Patrick, Dean Stanley, Capt. Condor and others.

In conclusion, the translator wishes to express his obligation to his father, Rev. Oliver Crane, DD., LL.D., for his kindly interest and encouragement throughout, and for many good criticisms and suggestions in revising the manuscript, and also to his friend Antun `Abdallah Salih of Beirut, Syria, for valuable assistance in interpreting certain obscure and corrupt passages in the original.

O.T.C.
Morristown, N. J.,
December 1889.

CHAPTER I.
IN THE NAME OF GOD, THE COMPASSIONATE.

This is the book narrating the chronicles of the children of Israil, from the time that our master Musa (Moses), the prophet- peace be upon him- the son of `Amran, invested Yush'a (Joshua) the son of Nun with the Kalifate over his people. All of this is translated from the Hebrew language into the Arabic language, after the manner of a rapid translation by word of mouth, and giving only the statement of the narrative, and nothing more: even what God- Powerful and Glorious- showed forth of signs and miracles and wonders, which man is too weak to adequately specify and describe; such as, what happened at the Urdun (Jordan), and also at the time when the giants were humbled, and with what victory and power and might and authority God came to his (Joshua's) assistance; also what they (the children of Israel) witnessed at the time of their entering the land, besides what they witnessed in Wady el-Mujib, and on mount Sina (Sinai) and its vast wilderness, with the essential incidents of this event which God made manifest, even the quaking of its mountains, together with what there was of thunders and lightnings connected with this, and joining the fires to the very heaven, and their hearing the code of their laws from the divine and eternal voice, from whom shone forth flashes of light, representing the form of its writer, even the Creator. Afterwards what happened to them at the greater Sea, not to mention what their adversaries witnessed in Greater Misr (Egypt), and what calamities overtook their enemies, such as Fir'aun (Pharaoh) and his army, and `Amlaq (the Amalekites) and its host, and Sihun (Sihon) and his kingdom, and `Uj (Og) the father of `Anaq with his sorcery, and kings of Mab (Moab) with their greatness. Also what happened unto Qarun (Korah) the son of the uncle of Harun (Aaron) and to the company who were with him, namely that some of them the earth opened its mouth and swallowed, and they went down alive to the deepest depths, while as to others of them the divine fire came forth and consumed their bodies. And also what happened to the people while they were in the wilderness forty years, suffering want, without a guide and with no provisions or clothing, and barely living and existing; whom the cloud overshadowed by day and the pillar of fire protected from cold by night, and whose food was the manna from heaven; and when there was need of water, our master Musa- peace be upon him- the son of `Amran, brought it forth for them from the rock and from the parched ground and stone, until they themselves had drank, and all that were in the company both living souls and animals. And it shall come to pass, that when they who are possessed of intelligence, but are yet unbelieving, shall have heard of what God did bountifully bestow upon them (the children of Israel), and with what happiness He did surround them, and how He lifted off of them all calamities, whether heavenly or earthly, and also what new things He revealed unto them, then they will know that, there is no Lord but their (the children of Israel) Lord and no prophet, but their prophet, and no book but their Book, and no true religion but their religion; and (they shall also understand) the excellency of the perfect creed, and the certainly of its validity, and that it is greatest in rendering praise to the Creator- Mighty and Glorious- the One who is omnipotent to do whatever He pleaseth. And when one shall hear of the decline of the kingdom of the children of Isrial, and what calamities and misfortunes and exiles and dispersions overtook them by reason of their disobedient doings and their rebellious actions, his fear will be increased for Him from Whom nothing escapes and of Whose kingdom nothing is destroyed- Blessed be he and exalted! And now of Him do we implore complete right-guidance and all-embracing favor in His mercy. Verily He is a hearer and answerer (of prayer).

CHAPTER II
THE ACCOUNT OF THE INVESTURE OF YUSH'A THE SON OF NUN WITH THE KHALIFATE OF THE PROPHET- PEACE BE UPON HIM.

At the completion of the hundred and nineteenth year, on the first day of the eleventh month, of the life of our master Musa the prophet- peace be upon him- God revealed unto him in the plain of Mab (Moab), that he should lay his hand upon the head of Yush'a, the son of Nun, the spiritual man; meaning by this, that he (Moses) should give him (Joshua) information of the profound secret, and revealed to him the vision of his dream and the science of knowledge, as much as he was capable of bearing; by the which his heart would be strengthened and his spirit perfected and his soul elevated, and the rule over the creatures (the children of Israel) be rendered easy unto him; and that he should also inform him of the Name, by which he should put to flight hostile armies, and by which a nation that no country could contain and whose numbers were countless might be confounded. And He ordered him(Moses) to set him (Joshua) before el-`Azar (Eleazar) the imam- peace be upon him- and to assemble unto him(Joshua) the people of learning and knowledge with the nobles and rulers, and ratify a compact with him, and make a new covenant with him, and invest him with the kingly authority, and install him in the rule over all the children of Israil. Thereupon the Prophet laid on el-`Azar the imam- peace be upon him- the command, which rested on him, to superintend the affair with completeness and splendor, and not to enter upon any affair or turn aside under any circumstance, except after he had seen to this. And at the completion of his inauguration, the priests sounded with trumpets, and the heralds made proclamation for his standard, and the banners and flags were unfurled to his reign. Our master, the prophet Musa- peace be upon him- had seen that he (Joshua) was wont to go forth in the front line of battle during his (Moses') days, in order that he might by actual trial gain experience of what he knew and had observed. And immediately he (Moses) gave command that, there should be selected out from the children of Israil- meaning by this, that there should be chosen from among them- twelve thousand men; from each tribe one thousand men; and thereupon he would with these make an attack upon the Midyanites, to take satisfaction for Israil out of them and their country. Now, before mention is made of the cause of this retaliation, we would remark, that the children of Israil had been restrained from intermeddling in any way with the affairs of the `Ammanites and Mabites, and were under orders not to appropriate to themselves any of their territory; and they did do only what necessity compelled them to do with them. Hereafter we will explain and elucidate this, by the will of God and his assistance, and the goodness of his guidance and favor.

THE SAMARITAN CHRONICLE

CHAPTER III
THE AFFAIR OF BILA'AM WITH THE KING OF MAB.

When the children of Israel went down into the plain of Mab, God revealed unto our master Musa, God revealed unto our master Musa, the Prophet- upon him be the most excellent peace- that he should not have anything to do with the `Ammanites and Mabites, nor should he wage war with them; "Because I," said God, "will not appropriate any of their lands to the children of Israil." And he (Moses) obeyed this and did accordingly. Now when it reached the ears of the kings of Mab and `Amman and Midyan what had happened unto Sihun and `Ug, of destruction and ruin and the taking captive of people and the talking of cities, forsooth they were sore distressed and feared exceedingly because of this; and they sent messages unto Bila'am, the son of B'aur (Beor), by men pre-eminent in sorcery and wisdom- for all the solders knew of him by reason of his invocations. And the delegates came into his presence, and said unto him: "The five kings of Mab and `Amman send unto thee their salutations, and say to thee: O, our master and our chief, we know that circumstances are brought about by thee, a knowledge of which the people of learning fall short of attaining unto, and that whatsoever thou blessest, is blessed, and whomever thou cursest, is cursed; and that thou canst put to route all armies by thy invocations and words. Now, perchance, there has already reached thee what has happened in Misr through the children of Israel, and in the sea and in the wilderness, and what happened unto `Amlaq, the chief of tribes, by reason of them, and what they did with Sihun and `Ug, and what they have resolved upon in reference to their permanent dwelling-places. And now their army has descended upon our border, and they are working for our destruction, and already they cover the face of the land; and we have come unto thee and hope to obtain relief of thee and security from them, through thy own free blessing and propitious aid, and also through what we have decided upon of happiness for thee, and the rendering of thy will absolute. Perchance now, our condition will be improved through thy agency, and thou wilt curse this people, and wilt prevail over them and effect a change in present circumstances through thy renown which is spread abroad, and the dignity of thy authority in consequence of thy circumstances, riches and servants; and there will be glory to us and to thee among all kings, in addition to what reward will be added unto this, in consideration for thy grand beneficence toward a people whom no country can obtain, and whose numbers are countless and beyond reckoning; for thou wilt have prevented a multitude from being murdered by fire. For the character and manner of this army is, that it is not restrained by a feeling of shame from an old man, nor does it accord protection to a woman, or have pity on a child, or show compassion toward an animal; for they do nothing else but murder with the sword, and stone to death with stones, and crucify, and burn with fire: yea, this is its custom, and it does not allow any mercy to be shown, or protection to be granted, unto any and it spares not even a leafless palm branch in its annihilating and destroying. By God, O our master, hasten unto us, bringing with thee whatever is necessary, and be not wanting unto us in this matter which involves the preservation of life, and we will reward a good deed with its like, and an evil deed with its like. And now, peace."

And when Bila'am heard this message, he made reply to the company of wise and trained men, and said unto them: "I will treat with due respect your rights, and the rights of those who urge you on in this message; but my action is controlled by the One whom I serve, if He gives me permission to go with you, I would accomplish your desire and the desire of those who urge you on in the message, and I would accomplish their (the children of Israil's) destruction, and in the end complete their annihilation, and would leave unto you a memory, for which you would praise me to the end of the ages. And now decide to lodge with me this night, and I will hear what shall be addressed unto me, and we will wholly act in accordance therewith, whether it be of good or evil." And the people consented, and lodged with him. And he began to offer worship to the One whom he was accustomed to serve, and it was said unto him: "Do not thou go with the people, nor curse Israil, for they are blessed." And he came to them with these words; thereupon they returned to the kings, and informed them of what had happened; but this only increased the more their desire after them, and this was high honor to him. And now there rode unto Bila'am more illustrious delegates than those who had gone before, and greater by far than they; yet they made less promises to him, and said in the second message: "Now see to it that thou comest unto us; for we are able to honor thee, and to give bountifully unto thee." Thereupon the people came unto him with this message; and Bila'am answered the messengers and said: "It is necessary that ye understand that, if the kings should give unto me their houses full of silver and gold, I cannot transgress what my Lord commands; but now abide this night with me, and I will hear what communication shall be addressed to me, and I will act in accordance with it, whether it be favorable or unfavorable." So the people lodged with him; and the man started in on the beginning of his performance and service and worship. God then desired to make a manifestation of His mysteries: now behold He could not do this Himself, nor could He do it through one who worshipped Him after the manner of anyone of the children of Israil, nor could He do it by writing, or by the agency of any of His angels, but forsooth only by sending unto him His very Command. And the companion of Bila'am upon beholding the spectre of the Command of God, fled away from it, and he became the visible form of the agent of the Creator who addressed Bila'am; for this was the device employed to communicate with him. And the Command of God said to him: "Did not I say unto thee, O Bila'am, when the people came unto thee; `go with them'?"; making inquiry to see what craving Bila'am had for the journey. But he answered him not a syllable, though his usual custom was to say: "Not so; for without my God I give ear to nothing." And he did not fully believe that he had heard the correct interpretation of the speech, until He commanded him to mount and ride, and then he was made to saddle his ass, and went along with the wise men of Mab. And the anger of the Creator was aroused, because of his starting out on the journey before he had sought instruction (of God), and he placed Himself in the way to make an attack upon him. Now he (Balaam) was riding upon his she-ass, and boasting of her before the people of learning, that he had no need of a guide when with her, and that he had no necessity ever to beat her. But when she espied the Agency of the Creator- Mighty and Glorious- standing in the way, with His drawn sword in His hand, she swerved aside out of the way through fear of Him; and this was the first of the putting to shame of Bila'am and of his remorse; and he beat her with his staff. And the Agency of the Creator removed to a place between walls in a field, and stood still; and when the ass behold Him, she shied into one of the walls and injured Bila'am's foot, and he beat her more violently. And when the learned and wise men beheld this, they said unto him: "O our master, it cannot be that there is a cause for her opposition to the execution of this mandate of the Divine Word?" And he answered and said unto them: "It was desired that this mandate should be carried out." And the Agency of God again passed on, until He stopped in a narrow place where there was no turning out either to the right or to the left; and when the ass beheld Him, she lay down under him (Balaam), and he again beat her violently. And God put speech on the tongue of the animal, and thereupon she said to Bila'am: "What have I done unto thee that thou shouldest beat me these three times? Am not I thine ass upon whom thou ridden since thou hast created up till now? Have I ever acted badly toward thee like as this time?" And he said: "No." Then God opened the eyes of Bila'am, so that he saw the Agency of God, even an angel standing in the way with His drawn sword in His hand, and he threw himself down before Him; and said unto him: "Why hast thou beaten thine ass three times? If thou hadst got right in front of me, I would have killed thee and saved he alive; for I have seen the wickedness of thy inclination. Now however, go along with the people, but keep carefully to what I shall say unto thee, and do not overstep it." Thereupon Bila'am journeyed on; and when the kings heard of his journeying, they came out to meet him, and they found him perplexed in his affair, and he informed them as to what had happened, and that in accordance with it he could not do anything except by the command of God- Mighty and Glorious. And the people took him to the cliff which is described in the holy Pentateuch, that he might behold all the children of Israil. Now after the man had been thus met and honored and made much of, his zeal was increased to obtain to the uttermost degree the love of the people. Thereupon he built on the cliff that has been described seven altars, and offered up on every altar a calf and a ram, and began to worshipping that he might hear what would be addressed unto him. And he heard what did not please him, and he announced what he had heard to the company of the kings; and they said to him: "Remove unto another place, and perhaps there the cursing of this place will be easier." And he obeyed them, and he did like he had done the first time, and he heard greater things than the first communication; and he began to go to the extreme in glorifying the children of Israil and honoring them. And the king of Mab said to him: "If thou dost not curse them, do not bless them." Then he besought them that he might remove unto another place, and he went and did as he had done the second time. And his eyes fell upon the desert and he saw the tribes of Israil, and divine spirits were guarding them, that is, the angels were protecting them every soul; and he turned away the evil eye from them, and hastened to glorify and bless them, until he said concerning them: "O Israil, cursed be he who curseth thee, and blessed be he who blesseth thee." And the anger of the king was aroused against him; but Bila'am said unto him; "Let not thine anger be aroused against me; did I not say unto thee that I could not act contrary to what I am commanded? But now assemble the kings with thee, that I may inform them your company of what will happen unto you and others besides you of the people, and I will give you information about a device, which, if carried out, will occasion their annihilation. Thereupon the kings assembled, and he made known unto them marvelous news, the explanation of which would be long; and he said to them: "Round about these people the holy angels keep guard, and the King of the heavens and the earth is with them, and it is not allowable to make use of sorcery against them, nor the science of astrology; nor will His heart repudiate them, except when they give themselves over to unbelief, or are led to do so by some stratagem, then the Creator will become angry with them and they will perish, and not a single one of them will survive."

CHAPTER IV.
THE ACCOUNT OF THE STRATAGEM AND ARTIFICE USED BY BILA'AM AGAINST THE CHILDREN OF ISRAIL

When the kings heard him relate what has preceded, they said to him: "How is the way to accomplish what thou hast mentioned concerning their destruction?" And he looked up the last resource of infidelity and pollution, and made it known unto them, and said to them: "Select of the most beautiful and fair women as many as ye can, and the king shall be the first to send forth his daughter with them; thereupon give unto each one of them an idol which she may worship, and an ornament which she may look at, and perfume which she may inhale, and food and drink; and the daughter of the king should be in a chariot which is wafted along with the wind, and it should be enjoined upon her that she make it her aim to go to the tabernacle, and pay her respects to no one except to their chief unto whom the crowd show deference, for he is their chief. And if in this she meets his approval, then she shall say unto him: " Wilt thou not receive me, or eat of my food and drink of my drink and offer sacrifices unto my god? For after this I will be thine, and with thee will do whatsoever thou desirest." For know, O king, that by the chief of this people being polluted, both he and his company will perish, and of them there will not remain a survivor." And the kings did what he recommended unto them; and there were collected to them twenty-four thousand girls, and they sent them away on the Sabbath day. And as they descended opposite the tabernacle, the chief of the tribe of Shim'aun (Simeon) rose up; for he was the chief of fifty-nine thousand men and was in the advance. And the daughter of the king advanced unto him, for she on beholding the great deference shown to him by his companions supposed him to be the prophet Musa- peace be upon him, and he ate of her food and drank of her drink and worshipped the idol which was in her hand, and after this she was submissive to him in his desire. Thereupon everyone of them- I mean this particular tribe- took one girl for himself; and the Creator became angry at the people, and destroyed of them in the wink of an eye four thousand men together with four thousand girls. And had not Finahas (Phinehas) the imam- peace be upon him- rushed from the presence of Musa the Prophet- peace be upon him- while he and his assembly were weeping at the door of the tabernacle, and seized in his hand a lance and bursting in upon them thrust through the man and girl- I mean the daughter of the king- and dispatched them, assuredly would the wrath of the Creator have destroyed the whole people; but by this action he removed and warded off the Divine anger from the children of Israil. And to Finahas- peace be upon him- there resulted from this noble fame and an excellent remembrance, and a covenant to the end of the ages. And praise be to God the Creator without cessation!

CHAPTER V.
THE HISTORY OF MIDYAN.

When the stratagem of Bila'am against the children of Israil was accomplished and there had perished of them this great number, and they had been overtaken by this calamity, God revealed to the prophet Musa- peace be upon him- that he should take vengeance for the children of Israil upon the people of Midyan, before that he should return to his elements (meaning by this, before his decease). So he commanded Yush'a the son of Nun, at the time of his investing him with his successorship, that he should go forth with the company which he specially mentioned, and with him Finahas, the imam, for he had gained the victory and a name, and he it was who had averte3d the Divine anger, and not anyone else, for he had hastened to obey his Lord. Now Bila'am had returned unto the king of Mab to congratulate him over the calamity of the children of Israil, and he found the kings collected together and indulging in joy and merriment, and before they were aware, 12,000 men had surrounded their city, whereupon they made haste in sending out the harlots with ornaments and censers and perfumes, taking for granted that what they had made a successful beginning in would be carried out to a perfect completion. But they (i.e., the Israelites) slaughtered these (the women) with the sword. Then Finahas- peace be upon him- with his cousin, went in advance and sounded with the trumpets, and the walls of the fortress fell down in ruins, and the army entered into Midyan, and they killed simultaneously the five kings and every man whom they found in it. And they began to make inquires about Bila'am, and they found him in a house of worship, and lo, he engaged in worship and was performing service. And they brought him out, and he was talking in speech that was unintelligible and could not be understood, because of the greatness of his confusion and bewilderment and the aberration of his mental faculties. And Yusha, the son of Nun, exerted himself to preserve him alive, that our master Musa- the peace of God be upon him- might behold him; but they of the tribe of Shima'un who beheld him were not obedient, nay, even, they cried out the Law against him, and put him to death. And Yusha said: "Who killed him? Why have ye done this, seeing we had taken him under our protection?" And they said unto him: " O our master, there should be no protection granted to an infidel, nor security to a sorcerer; had we not killed him, he might have effected the accomplishment of a stratagem against thee and against thy people. And we have dared to go contrary to thee in killing him, because of what was in our hearts concerning his deed, and if there be sin in our action in violating the protection accorded to him, lo, we assume it; but to our master belongs such exalted sentiments that he will look with liberality upon our excuse." And he approved of what they said and justified their action. And the people plundered Midyan, and drove away its cattle and took captive its women and children; and not a thing remained in it but they took it. And they returned laden with booty, victorious and safe; not a single man of them was missing. And our master Musa, the prophet- peace be upon him- with el-`Azar (Eleazar), the imam, the son of Harun (Aaron), and a crowd of chiefs went out to meet them. And when the beheld what there was among their number of captive women, our master Musa, the Prophet- upon him be the most excellent peace- became angry at them, and said to them: "This crowd has been the cause of your destruction." Thereupon he commanded them to kill every women who had known a man, and every boy child, and that none should remain except female children who had not known a man; and that they, together with the company that was with them, should separate themselves seven days for the purpose of purification. And they did so. And the number of the female captives who remained over after those who were killed, was thirty-two thousand girls; and of sheep there was 675,000 head, and of cattle there was 72,000 head; and of horses and mules and camels, 61,000 head; and of gold and silver and vessels and general goods, such a quantity as is impossible to define and describe. But, more wonderful than this, was the unharmed condition of the 12,000 men who entered a province such as this was, without the loss of a single man of them, or even one of them being overtaken by the bow of a sword or hit with a stone. Blessed be God, the One who is able to do whatsoever He pleaseth, and of Him do I ask assistance, and unto Him do I put my trust, and unto Him do I return penitently.

CHAPTER VI
THE ACCOUNT OF WHAT OUR MASTER MUSA, THE PROPHET-PEACE BE UPON HIM- EXPOUNDED, BEFORE HIS DEATH.

When God informed our master Musa, the Prophet, of the time when he could no longer remain alive, He commanded him to go up unto the mountain known as Nabah (Nebo). And he (Moses) proceeded to give instructions to Yusha, the son of Nun, and to the children of his brother, and to the assembly of the leaders, with regard to all necessary matters. And they remained with him some time, along will all the officers of the army and the people of wisdom; and he put them under a covenant that they would go with the children of Israil in the way which he had commanded them, and not swerve from it either to the right or to the left; and he ordered the priests to sound upon the trumpets, and send forth heralds who should proclaim throughout the congregation of the children of Israil: "Whoever desires to see our master Musa the Prophet- the most excellent, peace be upon him- let him come, that he may hear his blessing and whatever he shall reveal, and look upon him and bid him farewell, before he goes to the place which God has chosen for him." Thereafter he entered into the tabernacle and offered on the brazen altar the sacrifices, and lifted up the veil, even the veil of the holy house, and cast incense upon the golden altar, and worshipped his Lord; and then he bid farewell to the temple and what there was in it of omnipotence and divine majesty, and went out. And all the children of Israil according to their ranks were gathered together unto him, and he sat down upon an exalted seat, as was his custom, whereon he was elevated above the people and the light of his countenance shone as the rays of the sun. And he began to deliver an address unto the congregation of the children of Israil, in which he gathered together just as many as a servant of God could, of passages of praise to God, whose names are holy: and in it he expounded intelligence of the Divine favor which were to come, and the cause of Wrath and Error. And he informed the children of Israil concerning the deluge of fire, and the day of vengeance and reward, and defined the time of his return unto them. Then he announced unto them what should happen unto every tribe, and that would marshal them complete in the days of final perfection and completion. And he blessed them altogether, and they listened unto him. And, when the time came to bid farewell to each individual army, they began to cry aloud and wail and weep; and after a space of time he commanded them to be quiet and to sit down. Then he departed, walking slowly up the ascent of the mountain unto which God had ordered him to ascend, and with him were Yusha, the son of Nun, and el'Azar the imam, and the assembly of the leaders who were bidding him farewell and weeping at the approach of his separation from them and clinging to him. And when the farewells were prolonged with them, and night drew near, a pillar of divine fire descended and separated between them and their master- peace be upon him- and no one knows what happened to him after this, even unto this time. His allotted period of life had reached its limit, and the term of his existence among men- peace be unto him- and now his dealings were directly with his Lord and His angels. And of God do we beg that He would unite us to him through His mercy. Behold He is over all things powerful, and He is my sufficiency and illustrious Protector.

CHAPTER VII.
THE ACCOUNT OF WHAT YUSH'A, HIS DISCIPLE, SAID, AFTER THE DISAPPEARANCE OF HIS LORD AND MASTER.

When the master Musa, the Prophet- peace be upon him- disappeared from him and from the congregation of the children of Israil, and the COMMAND separated him from them, which event he was unable to avert from himself, and there passed away from them the sight of him, and when all had completely despaired of his return, Yush'a, the son of Nun, wept for him and proclaimed with his loudest voice, saying: "O Master! The death of every one of the children of Adam, from the first to last, was witnessed, and his grave seen; but thou! Who has seen thy grave? What prophet of the prophet can attain unto thy glory, or prolong his memory unto the extent thy memory is prolonged? Where is one who has brought to life the dead and caused the living to die, through the permission of his Lord, besides thee? Unto what prophet do the infidels bear testimony as to his prophetic office, except thee? What prophet, in the ages past or yet to come, did cause his congregation to hear the voice of the Creator from the regions of the heavens, except thee? Where is one who shall arise, and his words ascend on high and ward off the Divine anger, and bring down Divine mercy, except thee? What prophet fasted before his Lord, until he fasted one hundred and twenty days including the nights, except thee? What prophet boasted of his being the one who held converse with God without anything intervening between them, except thee? Where is one, who has trodden the fire, and cleft the darkness, and rent the clouds, and reached unto the curtain of omnipotence, besides thee? What book ascribed to any prophet has it the teaching of the worship of the Creator, and of how access may be had to Him, except they book? O one who killed the Nil (Nile) with his rod! O one who did reveal new things! O one who showed forth wonders! O one who manifested signs! O one who light up the darkness! O one who cleft the sea with his rod! O one-who put to rout armies with his hand! O one who warded off the Divine anger by his petitions! O one who brought down Divine mercy by his intercessions! O one whose very sustenance was the worship of his Lord! O one who went out from the boundaries of humanity and human power into the Divine power! O one who understood the past and knew what was to come! O one who ruled his enemies by his invocation! O my master and my lord! How can I exist and how can they people exist, now that thou art gone? After this his weeping increased as did also the weeping of the congregation that was with him, and when the grief and wailing had been long indulged in, with submission and humility, it was announced to Yush'a, the son of Nun, saying: "Return thou and those that are with thee of the army, and do not oppose the command of God"-May His name be glorious.

CHAPTER VIII
THE ACCOUNT OF WHAT WAS DONE AFTER THE
RETURN OF YUSH'A, TO THE PEOPLE.

When Yush'a, and the priests returned after bidding farewell to the prophet-peace be upon him,- the congregation of the children of Israil met them, and they commenced weeping for their master, yea, every company by company, and they continued weeping for him thirty days and nights. And the nations heard their clamor and wailing and crying, and they assembled together in confederation on the borders and rejoiced exceedingly when they were informed of the death of the prophet- peace be upon him, -and they resolved to encounter the children of Israil. But when God- Powerful and Mighty-perceived the conspiracy of the Canaanites, of those who were assembled unto them, He made a manifestation of Divine power and revealed unto Yusha, the son of Nun, that he should strengthen his own and the people's courage, by saying unto them: "That as He had been with them in the past, so would He be with them in the future so long as they continued in worshipful submission." Praise he unto Him to Whom belongs the kingdom and the majesty and the power and eternal existence. There is no God but He, and no kingdom but His kingdom.

CHAPTER IX
THE BEGINNING OF THE BOOK YUSH'A, THE SON OF NUN, THE DISCIPLE OF THE MASTER MUSA, THE PROPHET- PEACE BE UPON HIM.

After the death of Musa, Kalimu'l-lah, God made a revelation unto Yush'a, the son of Nun, the disciple of Musa, the servant of God, saying unto him: "O Yush'a, arise, start out, and with thy people pass over the Urdun (Jordan) unto the land which I am about to give unto the children of Israil; all the places which your feet shall tread shall belong to you. Your boundary shall be from the wilderness to el-Ludnan (Lebanon), and from the river el-Farah (Euphrates) unto the uttermost sea; and no enemy shall stand before you. O Yush'a, do not abolish the reading of what Musa the prophet inscribed and wrote, with what is intrusted unto the Liwanites (Levites) in the place in the holy house, and learn from it night and day, even all the days of thy life, that thou mayest be instructed; for if thou observest the same and dost not swerve from what is commanded thee to the right or to the left, thou wilt succeed and prosper, and thy enemies will be put to rout by thee, and thou shalt tread upon their necks." And at this time the communication ended.

CHAPTER X.
THE ACCOUNT OF YUSH'A ASSEMBLING THE CHILDREN OF ISRAIL, AND HIS RENEWING THE COVENANT WITH THEM

After Yush'a, had heard what God had revealed unto him, he joined unto himself el-Azar, the imam- peace be upon him- and he sat down upon his sacred chair, while Yush'a sat upon his royal chair. And there gathered unto them, the holy priests, and the Liwanites who offered the sacrifices, and the twelve chiefs who always attended them, and the chief judges, and the seventy chosen wise men, and the officers over the thousands, and hundreds, and fifties, and tens. And with the assembling of this congress, the trumpets sounded and the heralds went forth proclaiming a general assembling of the children of Israil. And it was not but an hour before there were gathered unto them the old men and the young, with many of the women and children and all the army. And then Yush'a, began to enumerate to them the things that God-Powerful and Mighty- had manifested by the hand of our master Musa the Prophet- peace be upon him- in their behalf and that of their predecessors. Next he recalled to them wherein they had acted contrary to Him, and tried Him, and rebelled against Him. And he said unto them: "O assembled men, I am going to bind you to the covenant and compact which existed before the death of the Prophet- peace be upon him- that you will not associate others with God, and that you will see to the promulgation of the laws upon which this covenant is founded, and it is, namely, the explanation of the law, and the explanation of what the obedient will receive and what shall befall the disobedient. And now this covenant in which I do confirm you is not with you and you alone, but includes you and those whom ye shall beget unto the end of the ages." And he told them what the other nations were wedded to, concerning the worship of idols; and informed them that God was with them as long as they remained in obedience, but that He would remove His favor from them upon their acting disobediently, and that then their ways would not prosper, nor would there be a united nation. Then he proclaimed in his loudest voice: "Assembled men, let there not be among you a disseminator of corrupt designs, spikes of corn and wormwood, (meaning by this, one who associates others with God and unites the worship of others with His worship); nor let there be among you one who cogitates in his heart wicked doctrines, or opposition to the command of God- Powerful and Mighty- lest there be a destruction of his mighty, holy nation and all its greatness, and separation from the Creator-may His name be holy- and your enemies attain unto their desires and plunder you of your cattle, and wives, and children. For whoever adopts these views, or any part of them, there shall fall upon him all the calamities which were written in the Holy Law, and God will blot out the remembrance of him under heaven, and will make him distinguished by reason of his calamities, apart from all the tribes of Israil. And so, be sincere with your souls and your conscience, that I may renew the covenant with you in accordance with what you may say; and God and His heavens and His earth, and His angels, shall bear witness against you in what happens between us and you; may the sentence be in your favor and not against you. And now if ye continue in keeping what has been commanded you, God- may He be blessed and exalted- will bless you and keep you and protect you and lead you to victory and will subdue your enemies and give the land, concerning which He swore, by His own omnipotence, unto your ancestors, Ibrahim, and Ishaq (Isaac) and Yaqub (Jacob)- peace be upon them. And He will keep you, and will keep the land in all happiness, and He will remove calamities and all disasters, and multiply you; but when ye shall have been disobedient and rebellious, the Divine favor will be removed from you; and the Divine power from your side, and from your support, and the angels will be removed from your side, and the name of the greatest King depart from giving you assistance, and there shall fall upon you those things which are written in the book of Wrath and Curse, and He will scatter your troops, and forget your affairs and the enemies will take possession of you, and there will remain no longer to you a king, or shrine, or possessions, or men, and God will disperse you throughout the regions of the earth from one extremity of it to the other, and He will make you servants and subjects. So now, whatever ye say and believe and covenant, let it be the real covenant binding upon you, and let this second covenant be added unto that which He covenanted with you through our master Musa the Prophet- peace be upon him. Therefore act sincere from your souls, and the secret thoughts of your hearts.

CHAPTER XI.
THE ACCOUNT OF HOW THEY ANWERED HIM, AND THE COVENANT THAT THEY ENTERED INTO AT THAT TIME.

The congregation of the children of Israil answered him, while crying out, weeping and humbling themselves before God, and casting their souls into His hands, saying: "O our master and our lord, we hear and will obey the command of God- Mighty and Powerful- and of His true and faithful Prophet, and also thy command, O king, and the command of our imam and our rulers, and there will be no opposition to what ye order, and no deviation from what ye say either to the right or to the left, nor from whatever our master Musa, the Prophet- peace be upon him- has ordained, and there shall be no rejection of a single part of it; and whoever shall rebel and deviate, and act treacherously, let upon him be the Curse and Wrath, for after this manner did our master Musa, the Prophet- peace be upon him- agree with us and impose conditions upon us, and put us under oath, and covenant with us, and offer up for us the sacrifices, and we answered him as we have answered you. And God is the witness over us in this, and He is our sufficiency and bountiful Protector."

CHAPTER XII.
THE ACCOUNT OF WHAT YUSH'A, THE SON OF NUN, DID IN ORGANIZING THE ARMY, AND THE MEMBERS THEREOF.

When Yush'a, beheld the zeal of the people he said, "The One who has insight into you and your purposes is God." And he renewed with them the covenant and compact, and offered for them the offerings, and the imam blessed them. Thereupon he and the imam, each of them, sat down on his throne; and he summoned the leaders, and demanded of them that they should make out a census of the children of Israil, tribe by tribe, and that the enumeration throughout the congregation, should embrace all men from the age of twenty years up to the age of fifty years, excepting the tribe of Lawi (Levi). And he ordered that this tribe should be enumerated, from the boy of a month old upwards: for so had our master Musa, the Prophet- peace be upon him- given orders before his death. But such as were under age twenty of age and over fifty years of age were not to be included in the enumeration. And the leaders made out the census, and the whole amounted to 601,730 men, although of this number the tribe of Rawban (Reuben), and the tribe of Gad, and the half tribe of Manashshah (Manasseh), had their landed possessions behind the Urdun (Jordan), even nine cities with their districts, which had belonged to Sihun and `Ug, the sons of Anaq; three cities and their provinces had been conquered by Nabih and his cousin of the tribe of Manashshah. For it did come to pass that, when our master Musa, the Prophet- peace be upon him- conquered these cities and destroyed their inhabitants, that there gathered unto him the leaders of these two tribes and a half, and they said unto him: "O our master and our lord, these cities suit us, for we have many animals and cattle, even though they be approximately less than one sixth of the assigned lands, while the whole number of the census of our men comes close on to one fifth of the army of the children of Israil." And he rebuked them, supposing that they preferred settling apart from their brethren. But they answered: "Behold we will leave our luggage and our cattle in these cities, and we will march forward under one enrolment, thrusting aside every pretext, and we will not return to our assigned lands until our brethren have got possession of all their assigned lands, and after that we will return unto our assigned lands and to our own places." And our master Musa, the Prophet- the most excellent, peace be upon him- answered them favorably, in reply to what they had asked of him, and assigned to them while he was alive this region. And the first of those whom Yush'a, the son of Nun, enrolled in his army, were the two and a half tribes, and the whole number of their enrolment was 110,580 men; and-according to these figures- the chiefs apportioned out the land from the Urdun to the sea. And this is the enrolment, based on the census, of the prosperous, victorious, holy, triumphant and blessed army. And the census of the tribe of Lawi was apart from the company of which mention has been made before; for the members of this tribe did not engage in the wars, nor did they separate from the service of their Lord; and the whole of their census, from a boy one month old and upwards, was 23,000 men. And when the leaders came with the enrolment of the census, Yush'a the son of Nun made them appear before him, and he announced good tidings unto them, namely, that God would bless them so as that there would result from one, a thousand as our master Musa the Prophet- peace be upon him- promised them from God- may His name be blessed.

CHAPTER XIII.
THE ACCOUNT OF THE SPIES WHOM YUSHA, THE KING SENT FORTH.

When Yush'a, the son of Nun, heard about the mustering of the Kanaanites, and the assembling of the giants, he sent out spies from the men of experience, intelligence, prudence and piety, to see the army of the enemies and make an investigation, and to proceed to Yar'ha (Jericho) and make an investigation as to the number of its men, and of those who were collected unto them, and then returning make it known to him. So the spies bid the army farewell, and invoked God's favor, and started out on their journey, having changed their outward appearance to the condition of ones who had come from far distant places. Now the spies knew all the languages spoken in the army of the enemies. And when they arrived at it they began to weep, and the enemy asked them, what news they had, and they said, "We are men from the people of the east, our companions have heard tidings of this great nation, which was for forty years in the wilderness without a guide or provisions, and the report reached our company that they have a Lord whom they speak of as `The King of the heavens and earth,' and that He has appropriated unto them both our country and your country, and so our companions have sent us out, that we may find out the truth of what has been reported unto us, and make it known to them. And we have journeyed and already passed by you a long time ago, while ye were busily engrossed in your occupations, and we did come to the army of that nation and found them perplexed, wandering round and round in the wilderness, and the secret among them was, that their God had become angry at them, and would not bring any of them into the land except two men; so we have returned with this good news, gladdened and rejoicing.

Now when it was so at this time that, we know what this nation had done with Sihun and `Ug, and with their lands and territories, and also what they did with the kings of Midyan and Mab, and the talking of their women and children and that this nation was bent upon entering your country and then our country, we made haste that we might make known to our companions the truth of this. And we journeyed unto them from the mountains, and we had but just reached the vicinity of the camps, when there came forth unto us three or four men, and each of them took hold of one of us, and fetched us into the presence of the new king, who had been invested with the kingdom as successor to Musa the Prophet- the best of peace be upon him. Now his companion was merciful who lifted not up his glance to any one; but this one was as a giant man, whose conversation broke souls, and whose speech split hearts, and whose reproach struck astonishment into minds. And we had but just stood in his presence when he knew our name and our origin and our country, and when we started out, and the places at which we had encamped, and in all that he mentioned unto us he was correct. And we at once believed in him and his Lord, through fear of him, but he answered us, that: This faith is not a faith to be accepted, when ye do so through fear; yet there is no fear for you; go, return and say to all whom ye meet and to your companions: Look out for your own welfare, and whoever flees away is safe, but whoever remains shall perish. For after the space of a week, the water of the Urdun will stand still for me by the command of our Lord- the Highest- until His people shall cross over; and not a fortress shall be shut in their faces, when they shall have gone around it seven circuits, for its walls will fall, and all they who remain, who are found inside, will perish: and the city and territory will be our territory, and the assigned lands shall become ours, assigned unto us by the King of the heavens and earth; whose creatures and servants all kings are. And this is the whole of what we heard from him, and we know that his name is Yush'a, the son of Nun, and that he is the one who put to route the Amlaq (the Amalekites), and is the slayer of Sihun and the destroyer of ʿUg, and the one who ruined the kings of Midyan and Mab. O woe to us and woe to you, and whatever is attached unto our country and your country; for they are a people who have no pity, nor do they leave survivors or show compassion, nor do they make a truce, except with those who are outside of us and you, for we stand, in their estimation, in the character of infidels and profligates and as a haughty and rebellious people; and the one who is lucky among us and among you is he who takes his own people between his hands and flees away with all speed, until he shall have got out beyond all their assigned lands, ere he feels regret where regret will profit him nothing." And the men rode on and pursed their journey, and after this manner did they speak with all whom they met until they returned to Yariha (Jericho), and here it became known about them, and they were sought after to be destroyed, and they begged protection of a woman who was called Rehab the innkeeper, whose house was beside the walls of the city, and she took them out and concealed them, and gave excuse unto those who sought them, saying, that they had already returned. Then she made a covenant with them and they with her, that, if God- Mighty and Powerful- should vanquish for them this city, they would spare her, and spare whatever souls were in her courtyard, of her own people. And the spies enjoined upon her to fix upon the roof of her house a sign which they should know, so that when she knew they were drawing nigh unto the city, she should display it; but they stipulated with her, that they would be innocent of the blood of all such as were found, of her own people, outside of the courtyard. And she brought them out, by night, and God willed their safe escape, and they returned to the army. And they told the king and the imam and their congregation, what they had witnesses and what had happened, what they witnessed and what had happened to them, and what favor the woman had done in their behalf. And the congregation answered them that they would spare the woman, in accordance with what they had covenanted with her. And the report of her spread abroad throughout the army, and the whole congregation of them knew her.

CHAPTER XIV.
THE ACCOUNT OF THE SUMMONING OF THE CHILDREN OF ISRAIL TO UNDERTAKE THE JOURNEY.

When Yush'a, the king, heard the statement of the spies, he sent forth the leaders, to proclaim throughout the army that they should proceed in the journey, having with them provisions for three days, and also to say in the proclamation: "O assemblies of men? Fear not, nor be dismayed, for God, your God, is about to journey with you, that He may show forth with you a miracle at this time, to make you successful over your enemies; and as to the miracle which God will show forth with you at the Urdun, the like of it has not been heard of in the ages past, now shall the like of it be heard of in the ages yet to come. And it is the first terror of you that shall fall upon the hearts of your enemies. Therefore, know, that the holy priests shall carry the golden ark, which is the ark of the covenant, which covenant is celestial substance, for it is the tablets whose writings was of Divine light: lo they are celestial substance; and when the priests with the ark shall enter the water of the Urdun, the water will stand still, and subside by the power of the ALMIGHTY, until that the water below flows away, while the water above shall mount up and increase upon itself, until all the children of Israil, and those who are in their company, shall pass over in absolute dryness."

The Yush'a, the son of Nun, himself called out and said: "O assemblies of men! God commands you that there should be between you and the priests who carry the ark an extent of equal space to two thousand yards, so do not approach unto it within this distance, that God may complete His work with you." The he ordered the twelve chiefs to take from under the feet of the priests, twelve stones, after that the children of Israil had finished the passage over the Urdun, and that each one of them should write his name upon his stone, in order that what had happened might be preserved and perpetuated through the eternity of the ages to come, even the miracle which God- may His name be glorious- would show on the Urdun. And the Liwanites (Levites) proclaimed with loudest voice: "Praise be to God of Gods, and Lord of Lords, to Whose commandments, animate and inanimate things are obedient, and the heavens and the earth and the seas and the rivers and all that therein is. There is no God but He, and no kingdom lasts but His kingdom, nor any power but His power, nor any sovereign except under His sovereignty. Perish whoever deny Him and believe in another than He, for He is the God.

CHAPTER XV.
THE ACCOUNT OF THE PASSAGE OF THE CHILDREN
OF ISRAIL THROUGH THE URDUN (JORDAN)

And the children of Israil did as the king commanded them. And the cloud was lifted up, on the first (day) of the first month, of the first year of the first period of seven years of the Jubil (Jubilee) even from the beginning of the entering in of the children of Israil within the boundaries of the assigned lands. And up to this time there had elapsed, of the days of the world as established by the law, two thousand, seven hundred and ninety-four complete years, and this reckoning of time is correct, which the learned know by chronological computations based on the era of the flood. And the priests proceeded forward when the cloud was lifted up, and attained to the distance from the army which he prescribed unto them. And when the priests with the ark approached the water of the Urdun, the Liwanites shouted aloud, and the congregation of the children of Israil joined in with them, saying with one voice; "There is no power or strength in the presence of Thy power, O Lord of worlds!" And the water stood still, and rose up in accumulation, by the power of its Creator; He who is almighty over whatever He wills, the Worker of miracles and wonders. And continued to be heaped up, wave upon wave, until it became like unto huge mountains, while the priests stood praising God, and shouting halleluiahs and saying: "Praise be unto Him, in obedience to whom every thing exists." And they stood, with the ark, on the dry ground in the midst of the Urdun, until all the children of Israil, with their large throng, and their cattle, had passed over on the dry ground through the midst of the Urdun, on its bottom, and it was dry like as in the days of harvest. And the Liwanites were praising and shouting halleluiahs, and saying: "Praise be unto Him in obedience to whom every thing exists. Praise be unto Him by whose will this is come to pass." And when the people came out of the Urdun they observed the commandment, and took the twelve stones from under the feet of the priests, and each man wrote his name upon his stone, and the king also took a similar stone. And when the priests with the ark came up out, the waters rushed down with great tumult, and winds blew violently with the rushing down of the waters. And the nations heard about this great miracle, and their hearts were broken up, and their confederated troops were scattered. And the water of the Urdun destroyed, at that time, many places which were near it, by reason of the great violence of the wind which accompanied it. And God does whatever He wishes- Glorious be His name. And of Him do I ask assistance, and upon Him do I put my trust, and unto Him be the praise for what He has bestowed.

CHAPTER XVI.
AN ACCOUNT OF THE HYMN OF PRAISE, WHICH YUSHA THE KING OFFERED UP.

Then Yush'a, the son of Nun, and the children of Israil offered up the hymn of praise, which our master Musa the Prophet- peace be upon him- offered up at the sea of el-Qulzum, and they added thereunto praises and halleluiahs, and rendered praise and thanksgiving for what God had generously bestowed upon them. And among the number of the hymns of praise which they offered up, they said: "Who is like unto Thee, O Thou who art perfect in holiness! O Thou who dost inspire terror! O Thou who dost reveal secret things! O Thou who dost perform new things! O Thou worker of miracles! O Thou displayer of wonders! How, O our Lord, shall we address Thee? O Thou revealer of signs! O Thou who makest light the darkness! Who is like unto Thee? There is no likeness like unto thy likeness, for Thou art the origin of actions and likenesses and bodies, and forms, and shapes, and spiritual things, which are endowed with the attributes of Thy nature." On that day Yush'a, the son of Nun, was magnified in honor among the children of Israil, and they feared him as they had feared Musa the Prophet- peace be upon him- and they knew that God was with him. And Yush'a, the son of Nun, set up twelve stones as a monument, rising up in the Urdun. And the chiefs erected the twelve stones in a place called Jalil (Gilgal), that the generations to come might behold them, and remember the drying up of the Urdun, and so praise to Doer of miracles; and that fathers might tell sons of this deed, and that kings and nations might hear that our God is the one conquering God. And when the kings of esh-Sham (Syria) heard of the children of Israil's crossing over into the land appointed unto them, and about the stoppage of the water of the Urdun, and its drying up, they arrayed themselves in funeral robes, and were smitten with fear, and some of them died through fear of the children of Israil, on account of the greatness of the awe which they inspired. And God made a revelation to Yush'a, the son of Nun, saying: "To-day have I spread awe of you and your people over these nations, and I have lifted off from thee, and from thy people, every impurity and infirmity." And Yush'a named the place Jalil, and it is its name unto the end of the ages. And praise be unto God, the One who endureth without cessation.

CHAPTER XVII.
THE ACCOUNT OF ANCIENT YARIHA (JERICHO), AT THE TIME OF ITS CONQUEST.

Upon the departure of the king from the place which he had named Jalil, they encamped in the district of Yariha, on the first day (of the feast of unleavened bread), the fourteenth day (of the first month). And they kept the Passover at this time, and ate unleavened bread from the new crops. And the manna ceased with their entrance into the land, and their eating of its crops, and of the fruit of its trees. And when the army had drawn near round about the city, Yush'a the son of Nun, retired apart from the camps, that he might worship his Lord by night, and when he had finished his devotions, he lifted up his eyes, and behold, the figure of a man standing, with his sword drawn in his hand, and he called out to him: "Yush'a!" Thereupon he (Joshua) replied: "Art thou of us, or of our adversaries?" And he answered him, and said: "I am the messengers of God, who rule over punishments." And he (Joshua) cast himself before him on the ground, because of his majesty. Then he rose up and said to him: "Lay upon thy servant the command which has been brought unto him." And he said unto him: "King, take off thy shoes from off they feet; for the place whereon thou standest is a holy place. God- Powerful and Mighty- says unto thee; O Yush'a, look before thee, behold I am about to place in thy hand this disobedient city, even Yariha, with its king and its people; now therefore choose for thyself, from among every tribe a thousand men. And they shall go round about the city, six circuits in six days, with the golden ark, the ark of the covenant, before them; and they shall not talk in conversation, or be intent upon anything except offering up praises and halleluiahs, nor shall they make an intermission in this, or raise any great tumult during the space of six days; yet the two priests shall be along with the two clamorous trumpets. But on the seventh day they shall go round about the city the seventh time, and the two priests shall sound with the two trumpets, and when the company hear the sound of the trumpets: then let them shout with a loud voice, three times, saying: `God is omnipotent in battles. God is His name.' And at the completion of this act, the wall of the city will be demolished, and the fortresses will fall down before the people, and the army shall enter the city and destroy it." And Yush'a returned and assembled the leaders of his people, and commanded that they should select twelve thousand men. And when they came unto him, he gave orders to them to march, and with them should be the sintly priests, bearing the ark and two trumpets. And he gave instructions unto the company, that they should offer up halleluiahs and praises, during the six days, in a low tone of voice; but on the seventh day they should round about the city six times, "And on the seventh time around the priests shall sound the trumpets, and upon their hearing the trumpets, the whole army shall shout with a loud voice, and instantly advance: and then the fortifications will be demolished, and God will put the city in your hands. And when this has been successfully accomplished by you, and ye have attained the city, ye shall put to death every breathing thing which ye find in it, whether of men or animals. And ye shall destroy it and burn it, and shall not leave in it any, except the woman who is known as Rahab the innkeeper; her ye shall spare, and also those souls that are in her courtyard, according as the spies made covenant with her. O assemblies of Men! Be watchful of yourselves; do not take anything from the city; burn its gold and silver and brass and iron, and all its appurtenances, and do not meddle with anything that is devoted; for then would ye and the army perish." And the people did as he instructed them. And on the seventh circuit the priests sounded with the two trumpets, and they cried out with a great shout; and at that, the walls of the city fell down, and the army entered in, and put to death every breathing thing in it from man even to animals. And they collected all the furniture which was in it, and placed it in the middle of the city, and burned it, and it became a mound never to be rebuilt. And Yush'a proclaimed in the loudest voice; " O assemblies of men! It is forbidden unto you, and unto those who shall rise up of your seed, to build up in this city one single stone." And it is the first of the rebellious cities, known as Ancient Yariha; and this city was devoted, destroyed, burned and converted into a mound, never to be built up or restored, throughout eternal ages. And this was done after the spies had entered the courtyard of the woman, and brought out her and every soul that was in her courtyard, and preserved them from death. And the name of Yush'a, by this act of his, was spread abroad unto the different regions of the earth. And a man of the children of Israil committed a trespass, and entered into the temple of the idols of this city, and he found therein a goodly thing of gold, and tongue of gold, their weight was two thousand, two hundred and fifty mithqals, and he took them and concealed them in his tent; now it had been forbidden him to even touch it, not to mention his taking it in theft, and hiding it in his place of abode. And the Lord became angry with the children of Israil, on account of him. And neither the leaders nor the king knew about this deed. But praise be unto Him who knows secrets, and who shows forth miracles. Blessed be His name, and exalted be His fame.

CHAPTER XVIII.
THE ACCOUNT OF THE DISCOVERY OF THE ONE
WHO TOOK THE DEVOTED THING.

When it was morning of the day of which mention has already been made, Yush'a the king, and all the army, came before the temple, and he made chiefs present themselves before el'Azar, the imam- peace be upon him,- and upon him were the jewels. And the jewel which was inscribed with the name of Yahudah (Judah) grew black; and he, in succession, presented the tribe of Yahudah, in its companies, name by name, before the jewel; and it grew black at the family of Zarah (Zerah), the son of Yahudah, And the man at once presented himself and stood before Yush'a the king. And the king said unto him: "O man! Lift up thy face to the King of the heavens and earth, and know that He knows secrets, and, O, woe be to the one who imagines that he can conceal from Him anything, or cover up from Him a matter. So now confess as to how you have sinned, and what you have taken of the devoted thing; for God has become angry with His people on your account." And the man answered him, and said: "I know, O king, that I have committed a great sin before God, Who knows what is secret and concealed, and I have been a traitor to the covenant of God, and of His messenger; for I entered the temple of the chief idol of Yariha, and there found a goodly thing of gold, and tongue of gold, and their weight was two thousand and fifty mithqals, and my soul became greedy for this, and I took it and buried it in my tent. And now if a crime like mine can be pardoned, well and good, seeing that God is merciful and compassionate; but if there is no pardon for it, then let there be executed what thou shalt command in my affair." Then the king sent immediately trustworthy people, and they brought what the man had mentioned he had felt greedy after, and so had taken it. And the governor and his associates, the chiefs, brought him before the temple of the creator, and command was given that he should be burned outside the camp. And he took the man and burned both him and whatever children he had, and cattle, and all that he possessed, and he placed all in a deep valley, and commanded the whole army to stone it with stones. And he named the valley: The valley of `Akur (Achor). And after this God removed His anger from the children of Israil; for what they did appeased Him. And unto Him be praise; for His bounty and the excellency of His favor and goodness.

CHAPTER XIX.
THE ACCOUNT OF HOW CERTAIN PEOPLES OF THE KANAANITES PRACTICED A STRATAGEM, AND OBTAINED PROTECTION OF THE KING.

After the capture of the city, the king and his people returned unto the place which was named Jalil. And they took no notice until there came unto them a company of men, whose faces were blackened, and their garments and shoes worn out, and with them was bread that had become putrid. And they approached unto the king and unto the chiefs of the children of Israel, in this place, and saluted them, as the like of them were wont to salute, and they prostrated themselves before the assembly; then they said to the king: "We seek protection of thee and of thy people, that we may exist in your company; for we are of those who choose for ourselves, God your Lord." And he answered them: "Verily I will not grant protection unto you, unless ye inform me who ye are and from what place ye come." And they answered him: "We are people from a far distance, we have heard of your fame, and what signs and wonders God- Powerful and Mighty- has revealed to the children of Israel, even in the sea, and in the desert, and in Wady el-Mujib, and what has happened unto the kings through you. And now, O king, we have repaired unto thee that we might be in the company of those who beg protection with thee; for we believe in thy Lord, and we will not resist whatever thou shalt prescribe unto us, be it small or great. And behold thou seest our blackened faces, and our worn-out clothes, and our dried-out food; for we did not start out from our places, to come here in garments of old clothes, but this is the necessary result after the long journey. And now trust us with protection, that we may exist in the company of this great, blessed, holy people." And Yush'a bid some of his people advance unto them, and he entered into a covenant with them, and swore unto them by the God of Israel, that they would not kill them, nor those who were members of their company. And when it was after three days, the king found out that, that they were of his enemies, from three towns near him, on the south of the blessed mountain, and they were: Jaba'un (Gibeon) and Qiryah (Kirjath-jearim), and Birut (Beeroth). And no one of the army was able to go to this place, because of the protection granted, and the oath, and covenant. Thereupon the king summoned the men, and said unto them; "Why did ye conceal from em, and say that ye were from a distance, while ye were neighbors?" And they answered him, and said: "We knew that the God of the children of Israel, had commanded you to destroy these places, and not to spare the sword in any place in which a soul was, and we feared for ourselves, and did what we did; and now we are in thy hands, O king, do with us whatever you decide upon." And he set them at liberty, and make proclamation throughout the children of Israel, saying: "Do not kill them; but they shall become among the class of those cutting wood and drawing water for the beasts." And they did this with them, according to what he commanded.

CHAPTER XX.
AN ACCOUNT OF THE KANAANITES, WHOSE TERRITORIES THE LAND WAS.

Some of the Kana'anites, when they heard of the children of Israil's passing over the Urdun, had fled to one people and another; but when they had been informed of what had befallen Yariha and its people, all those who were dwelling around Urdun, and the great sea, gathered themselves together, and entered into an agreement, and made preparation to meet the children of Israil, and join in battle with them. And the sent five of their chiefs, with the majority of the army with them; and they were bidden to advance and make an attack upon the three towns which had sued for themselves protection with the children of Israil. And they began with Jaba'un and put its people to great straits. And the inhabitants of Jaba'un sent unto Yush'a, the king, to inform him of the truth concerning the intentions of the kings, and that they had already commenced by destroying them, and that they were now in a state of severe siege and extreme distress; and they pled their cause with him with the greatest emphasis, and begged him to deliver them from this enemy, who was carrying out the designs against them. And while they proceeded on their journey, the king collected his assembly, and God made a revelation to him in that night, saying: "Do not fear, O Yush'a, behold I am about to give over into thy hands these five chiefs; do not let a single man of them, or of their soldiers, escape safe." So he marched forward and surprised the army of the enemies by night, and the watchword of the children of Israil was GOD THE OMNIPOTENT IN BATTLES, GOD IS HIS NAME. And the five kings were driven in flight before them unto Kasahah, and unto Maqadah (Makkedah). And when the children of Israil came up with them, they conquered them, and did not spare in killing them. And Yush'a spoke unto the day to stand still, and it stood still; and the day was great, for God heard the voice of the children of Israil, and sent forth the angels with them. And the five kings, the chiefs already mentioned, fled and found a cave in Maqadah. Then the king ordered to place great stones on the mouth of the cave, that he might keep them under guard, until they (the children of Israil) should return, when they have made an end of destroying the rest of the army. And he killed the multitude of the people, and not a single man of them did escape safe. Then they returned to the cave, and the king gave command to bring them (the five kings) out, and to throw them down upon their faces and ordered the prominent leaders of the army to tread with the soles of their shoes upon their necks; and he said to the children of Israil: "Be strong and of good courage, and fear not, nor be dismayed, for thus shall God do with your enemies." The he gave command that the kings should be killed, and be crucified until the setting of the sun; and after sunset he gave orders, that they should be placed in the cave to which they fled, along with the wood upon which they had been crucified, and also that there should be placed over the mouth of the cave, a mound of stones, to perpetuate the knowledge of this unto the end of ages. And they did what he ordered, and the, being gladdened, assembled together.

CHAPTER XXI
THE ACCOUNT OF THIS ARMY, AND ITS TRIUMPH, AND THE DESTRUCTION OF ITS ENEMIES.

When it was the beginning of the eight month (now this is the time of the journeying of this army), the king divided the infantry and cavalry into three bands, and sent each band in a different direction, while he and they who were with him journeyed along in the highway, tending towards the hostile people; and he first alone was the one who surprised the enemies' camp, and he held them for a considerable time in an engagement, and they were not as yet recovered from the surprise, when there arose a cloud of dust, and the army approached from every side. And when the children of Israel behold one another, they shouted out with loudest voice: God is our Lord, who wages instead of us the war." And God on that day showed miracles with the enemy, for it came to pass that every one who would flee fire met him and burned him up. And a spectre appeared among them, so that the horses did stampede with them, upon hearing the shouts of the children of Israel and carried them down to death; and the hours of the day were lengthened out for them, as God had promised them, until they had accomplished in it the results of a whole year, and not a remnant in it the results of a whole year, and not a remnant of the enemies was left after this battle. And the king from Mahzun wrote a letter unto el-Azar, the imam, binding it on the wing of a bird; telling him in it the good news about what God had bestowed upon them, and what He had shown forth among them of miracles and signs, which should be eulogized. And he also informed him that he would not return until he should have taken possession of the remaining territorial districts for the children of Israel. And he set the bird at liberty on the mourning of the fifth day, and it immediately proceeded on its journey, under the blessing of God and the goodness of His guidance and grace.

And he (Yush'a) continued descending upon one city after another, and taking possession of them, and doing with the rebellious like unto what we have already mentioned, until he had completed the subjugation of the territories, and then he returned in the first month of the second year. And it resulted, that he, in one year, took possession of all their territories, and this was the region of the seven Kana'anites, whose fame is enduring, well known and spread abroad. Then he and all who were with him removed apart for purification; now there descended from the blessed mountain a great river which watered the lowlands, and to it the king went down with all his army. And when he had completed his purification, el-Azar the imam offered up for the sacrifices, and they celebrated a grand feast, the carrying out of which was complete and consummate. Never was there witnessed a better feast than it; for the people were united, not having as yet dispersed throughout their territorial sections, and when they did shout, and praise, and exult with halleluiahs, they were heard in the most distant and remote places. And when the feast was over, the king and his assembly gathered together, and began to arrange the distribution of the territories among their people; and they asked God, Mighty and Powerful, for His favor and guidance.

CHAPTER XXII.
AN ACCOUNT OF THE APPORTIONMENT OF THE TERRITORIES BELONGING TO THE CHILDREN OF ISRAIL, AND THEIR BOUNDRIES.

The king selected men from the geometricians and their associates, and from the land surveyors, and those who were well skilled in matters pertaining to lands, and from those who were assisted in surveying, and those who were expert in estimating. And he gave instructions that they should divide it into ten parts; and he himself set about equitably distributing the nine and one half tribes over the ten sections. Thereupon he defined unto them the boundaries of the lands, according to what our master Musa the Propet- peace be upon him- explained in the chapter of the boundaries, which is mentioned in the Law, where he says: "When ye come into the land of Kana'an (and this is the land that shall fall unto you for an inheritance, according to the boundaries thereof), then your south quarter shall be from the wilderness of Sin along by the places of Edum." And this is the boundary of the lands of the two and one half tribes. And then he again says: "And your boundary on the south shall be, from the furthest eastern part of the salt sea unto the side of Misr (Egypt); and the goings forth of this boundary shall be at the gulf." That is, from the isthmus of the wilderness; by which is meant the land of el-Hejaz (Arabia), and esh-Sham (Syria), and the pass of Haljat (?), a narrow place which reaches to the sea (the Arabah). And the going forth thereof shall be southward of Quds-er-Raqim"; meaning thereby, to the south of a place called Quds-barna (Kadesh-barnea), upon the bonders of esh-Sham and el-Hejaz; for the idea held by the people of that time was to the effect that it came unto el-Khaq (?) until it reached unto the Nil of Misr (Nile of Egypt), which is the valley whose going forth are to the sea, the coast line of which extents from Misr to Falastin (Palestine) and to er-Rum (Greece). "And your western boundary shall be the last sea." And the last sea is from Misr unto esh-Sham. "And the border towards esh-Sahm extends from the great sea to the mountain el-Jabal (Mount. Hor) and to Ainan of Hums (Hazar-enan)." The king here meaning the bend in the mountain el-Libnan (Lebanon), as far as the limit of its land in the district of Dimashq (Damascus), until coming eastward it goes around it, and returns sloping downwards unto the Urdun, and its goings forth are unto the salt sea, which is the final point designated in the beginning of the chapter. "And this," (said Joshua) "is the smaller part of the assigned land but they (the surveyors) shall make a return on the half of the greater assigned territories, according to the sum of the census of the nine and one half tribes." Then he instructed them that they should set apart forty-eight cities, out of all the territories of the children of Israil, unto the

Liwanites, taken out from the divisions; and from their total number there should be six cities of them (even three cities from the whole number of the cities of the two and one half tribes, and three cities form the whole of the assigned lands of the nine and one half tribes), concerning which cities God-Mighty and Powerful- gave command that they should be set apart, and he named them; "Cities of repulse"; that is, of refuge to the one who flees thereunto, even to the one who should kill his companion inadvertently, that is, by accident, or through carelessness, without intention, or malice aforethought; so would these cities be a repulse to the avenger. And the slayer shall not be killed until he shall have stood before the judge and the assembly of the leaders; and now if he did kill intentionally, he shall himself be killed; but, if it was through carelessness, then he shall flee unto some one of these cities, and he shall not go forth from it until the chief imam dies; and if he do go forth outside of the boundary of this city, and the avenger meet him and slay him, then shall he be innocent of his blood. And the men (that is, the geometricians and the estimators and they who ere skilled in matters pertaining to lands) started out on their journey, according as they had been commanded.

CHAPTER XXIII.
THE ACCOUNT OF WHAT YUSH'A DID UNTIL THE SURVEYORS RETUNED UNTO HIM.

After this the king assembled the two and one half tribes before el-Azar, the imam- peace be upon him-and the leaders; and they thanked them for their deeds and the help and assistance they had rendered, and said unto them: "Ye have zealously observed the covenant of God and the covenant of our master Musa- the best of peace be upon him- and there now no longer remains to us an argument against you; for verily, ye have acted kindly, and have preserved life and borne hardships, and have been patient in abstaining from visiting those whom ye have left behind, until your brothers have gained their goal in taking possession of their assigned lands. And now your standing is exalted, and your deeds grow before God your Lord, who is the rewarder of good deeds, with their like a thousand- fold; and ye have got possession of your assigned lands, which are most excellent for your people, and in them ye have no opponent or oppressor. And these are our wishes of good fortune to you in it: may God multiply unto you in addition to it, its like." Then he gathered together their prominent men, and invested them with robes of honor, and gave presents unto them. And he commanded them and enjoined upon them, to go over the list of the census; and they did this, and not a single man of them was missing. And they did eat and drink together, and renewed the covenant between them, that they would remain in obedience unto God always, and in the love of His Prophet, and keep His commandments; and that they would come to the support of one another whenever any tidings should reach them, whether by night or by day, in ease or in distress, in joy or in sorrow; nor would they have a falling out with each other, nor pretend to be asleep; but, on the contrary, would vie with one another in showing haste and speed. And they proceeded to bind themselves unto this with a great oath. And el-`Azar, the imam- peace be upon him- offered up for them the sacrifices, and then the leaders of the congregation of the children of Israil gathered together to bid them farewell. Thereupon the king appointed as king over the 110,580 men (which was the number of the two and one half tribes), Nabih (Nobah)the son of Jil'ad (Gilead), of the tribe of Manashehah, and invested him with the royal robe, and placed upon him a crown, and had him ride one of his chosen horses, and sent forth before him a herald, proclaiming: "This is the king of the two and one half tribes, who is invested with their judicial matters, who shall oversee their affairs; the chief leader of their army; the chief orator among them; the one who shall be asked concerning their affairs and every judgment of his shall be carried out, and in whatever matter of judgment to el-`Azar, the imam- peace be upon him. O assembled men! Whosoever shall oppose his decree, or withdraw from obedience to him, the blood of this one can be shed, and all the people shall be innocent of his crime." Then he delivered unto him a copy of the book of our master Musa, the son of `Amran the Prophet- peace be upon him- and he enjoined him to read it night and day, and informed him that in it were marvelous indicatory signs, showing how life may be prolonged in this present fleeting world and in the world to come, and also that in its reading was protection from spirits, and the evil eye, and calamities, and witchery, and the skill of the enemy. And he gave over to him twelve tribes, whom he commanded to adhere unto him and not leave him, until he should have corresponded with every chief of a tribe resident at the court of the king and the saint of God; and he also selected for him men from the learned, who might ease him in the administration of the government, and whom he might consult in important matters which unexpectedly arose to him. And, moreover, he gave over to him two thousand men of the Liwanites, who should take up their residence in the cities that had been set apart unto them among these tribes, and these should receive the portion of God, and the portion of His saints: tithes and votive offerings; and should perform whatsoever sacrifices were incumbent upon them in every month, and should execute the judicial sentences in the presence of their leaders, and should establish prayers for them, and oversee the matters which it is unlawful for any body else but them to do. Thereupon the banners were unfurled before him (Nabih) and the trumpets sounded, and the saint of God and the king (Joshua) rode out with their assembly to bid them farewell; and it was a great day, the like of which it was not possible could have existed in the world. And they proceeded on their journey under the protection of God, victorious, triumphant, happy and rejoicing. And when the news reached their friends who were watching over their affairs on the other side of the Urdun, their assembly came out to meet them. And Nabih divided out that region according to the sum of the number of his companions. And the Liwanites entered into their places, and attended to the offering of praises and halleluiahs. And glory be to God, for His bountiful favors unto them.

CHAPTER XXIV.
THE ACCOUNT OF THE RETURN OF THE MEN WHO WERE EMINENT IN MAKING SURVEYS AND ESTAMATING JUST PROPORTIONS, UNTO YUSH'A, THE SON OF NUN, THE KING.

After the return of the geometricians, and those who were trained in surveying the land out into fields and equitably proportioning them, and in rendering correct judgments as to their trees and everything that would hinder their cultivation, the king and the twelve chiefs assembled together. Now these were they to whom our master Musa the Prophet- peace be upon him- had given instructions that they should unite with him in dividing out the land; with the restriction, however, that no one should obstinately oppose him, nor should any quarrel or dispute occur between them; and they began to arrange the division of it into ten parts, and distributed the tribes over the ten parts according to the greater or less numbers a tribe had, until they had equalized all this. And when they did come to an agreement with regard to it, they permanently settled it and perfected it, and clearly set forth; and when the opinion of the assembly was agreed as to the rectitude of this, they brought up the lists unto the saint of God, the imam el-`Azar- peace be upon him- and when he had carefully perused it, he wrote it, he wrote with his own hand a copy of the distribution and divisions of the tribes. Thereupon he wrote ten tickets, inscribed on which were the parts of the distributions and of the assigned lands, and he wrote the name of each one of the parts of the tribes upon a ticket, and gave unto each several chief his ticket. And then each chief went apart with his people and assembled the leaders of his followers, and divided out every part according to the sum of the census, to every man according to the size of his family. And with every one (of the chiefs) there went forth some of the geometricians and surveyors to equitably arrange matters among them. And the district embracing the excellent mountain fell among the assigned lands of Yusha the king, the son of Nun, and of his comrade Kalab (Caleb) the leader of the whole tribe, and with which he had started out on the journey (from Egypt) in company with him (Yusha). Thus was every one permanently located in his place. And he (Yusha) distributed some of the Liwanites, every one in the place which had been set apart for him out of the whole of the assigned lands, over and above the division, that they might administer the affairs of the people in reference to prayers and judicial matters, and also receive the tithes and perform the sacrifices. And he assigned unto each tribe chief-justices who should correspond with the imam, and give him information of what happened in their districts. Then Yusha the king built a fortress on the mountain to the north of the Blessed Mount, which (fortress) is known as Shamrun (Samaria). And this wont was to visit with el-Azar one day in each week; and one day with the learned, that he might take counsel with them; and one day with the chiefs, that he might inquire into their affairs; and one day he spent in attending to his own business and matters; and on three days he left not the book of God, during night and day. And this was his method in his administration of government, when he was not out waging war; for he did not hold himself aloof from them. And he built a synagogue on the summit of the Blessed Mount, and collected and kept in it the tabernacle of the Lord, and no one, after him, did hold it, except the priests and the Liwanites.

CHAPTER XXV.
AN ACCOUNT OF THE CIRCUMSTANCES OF THE CHILDREN OF ISRAIL AFTER THE DISTRIBUTION.

Then the children of Israil began to inhabit their assigned lands and to put them under perfect cultivation, and to worship their Lord with acceptable service, and to fulfill on each day whatsoever sacrifices were incumbent upon them. And God showed forth with them blessings and watchful care, so that calamities were removed away from them; and not a single one of the kings of the enemies did have power to do any violence unto them. So that there was a multitude of their own travelers journeying from every province unto the Blessed Mount three times a year, along with various kings, with wealth and joy and gladness; and not one of the enemies dared even to look towards them, or stand up in opposition to them. And the king and the leaders and the whole army continued in rest and tranquility for a period of twenty years. There was no molestation or insurrection since now their surrounding enemies were far removed from them and dispersed throughout the regions of the earth; and they who were near them had made peace with them, so no one was stirring up a commotion, nor was there a kingdom spreading itself abroad except their kingdom, or any hand outstretched except their hands. And not a single day did pass but that they hears news of all their companions; and thus did they continue to have intelligence of them, until this period came to a close. Then after this there happened those things which by the will of God, and His assistance, we will narrate and explain. (To Him be the praise.)

CHAPTER XXVI.
IN THE NAME OF GOD, THE COMPASSIONATE.

HAMAM, the son of R'awan, king of the Persians, had been put to death along with all the kings whom Yush'a had killed, then his child grew up. Who was known by the name of Shaubak, and he was eminent in attainments and in the acquisition of wealth. And he began corresponding with kings throughout all the regions, puffing some of them up, and stirring up others of them to anger, and influencing some of them by promises, and conciliating others of them with gifts of riches. Thereupon he said, that he wished to take revenge for the murder of his father. And he also corresponded with the survivors of the Kana'anites, and recalled to their memory what the children of Israil had done with their children, their wives, their cities, and their possessions. Then he sent also unto the king of Arminiyeh (Armenia) the Greater, and Rumiyeh the Less (Asia Minor). And he joined unto himself the son of Yafet (Japheth) the giant, and also sent unto the king of Sida (Sidon) and of el-Qaimun, and to the king of esh-Sham (Syria), making known unto them what army had been assembled together unto him, and agreed with them that they should assemble together at el-Qaimun. And the opinion of the chiefs of the army and its leaders were agreed that they should send (as spy) a clothing-merchant, who should count the men, and inform himself as to the army (one who was clever in prudent management), in order that he might make known to them the condition of the children of Israil, and how was the way to them and the means of getting at them. And they resolved to write and forward by his hand a letter from their company to Yush'a the king, so that they might obtain security from him, seeing he acted as a messenger, for upon a messenger rests no crime and hence no fear.

CHAPTER XXVII.
STATEMENT OF A COPY OF THE LETTER WHICH THE GIANTS SENT UNTO YUSH'A THE SON OF NUN, THE KING.

The letter began:

"From the assembly of the giants, the confederated, well-known, far-famed, victorious, triumphant, mighty in courage, protected from armor, and the foremost of all mortals; to Yush'a the shepherd, the son of Nun, and his people. Peace from us unto you.

We know, O murdering wolf, what thou hast done in the cities of our associates, and that thou hast in murder destroyed all of their leaders and sent them down to the bottom of the lowest depths, and hast demolished the places in which there was for us aid, and hast put down the provinces which were our supports and from which our helpers were ever providing themselves with food, and hast destroyed for us thirty cities, besides residences and small towns, and that thou didst not reverence old men, nor have compassion upon little infants, nor didst thou give ear unto them and grant them protection, nor leave a place unto those begging safety of thee. Nor grant time for good action. And the reason of this (thysuccess) was, that then we were distracted by discords and dissensions, and a lack of unity in our counsels; but now understand, O murdering wolf, that we are coming unto you with all the kings in harmonious agreement, with spirits in concord, and tongues that have pledged mutual covenants, and hands that have been struck together. With conditions all-perfected, and souls full (of wrath) and accumulated complaints, and livers, as it were, cut asunder, whom no stampede can ever overcome, nor a great fire put to fright.

And now after thirty days we will bring on the battle between us and thee in Merj Balata, in front of the mountain upon which thou worshipest they Lord, which is referred to as the Mount of Blessing. And there will be no delay on our part, or on the part of any one of us; so be prepared for those whom thou shall meet, and make no excuse for thyself by saying that thou art taken by surprise, or that the enemy came against thee by night. And, moreover, know that in our company there are thirty-six kings, and in the army of each king sixty thousand knights, besides foot-soldiers innumerable and countless, who make sport of devices (employed); and there is also with us the son of Yafet the giant, who has with him a thunderbolt of steel, and when he hurls it, and it is granted full success, it kills a thousand men, and when full success is not granted, it kills five hundred men; and they who are with him are kings, and with them are instruments and implements of war, which they have inherited from their grandfather Nuh (Noah)- peace be upon him. Therefore take knowledge of this and act in accordance therewith, and look out for thyself, for thou art about to be brought to account for what thou hast done. And now peace."

And the messenger took the letter, and proceeded on his journey at once. And they began to draw up the army and arrange it in order, and set out upon the journey to el-Qaimun, that they might unite with their confederates whom they had summoned by letter to be present.

CHAPTER XXVIII.
THE HISTORY OF THE MESSENGER, AND WHAT CAME OF HIM.

The messenger executed his orders on the tenth day of the second month of the twenty first year of the reign of the children of Israil, after their entrance into this territory: and he arrived on the fifth day (of the week), the morrow being the day el-Miqra (the Convocation), that is the feast of weeks. And he handed his letter unto the king, as he was sitting upon his royal throne pronouncing sentences upon such of them as were worthy of death, and such of them as deserved to be burned, and such of them as deserved to be stoned, and such of them as deserved to be imprisoned; for important cases were referred up to him at the time of the feasts, and then judgment was passed upon these in accordance with the light of God and the command of His saint. And he (Yush'a) did not turn towards the messenger until he had concluded his judgments, and had finished rendering his judicial decisions at the end of the day, then he took the letter, and read it at his home, and not a single person knew about it until his feast had passed by, and so the people did rejoice during their feast; but he himself was distracted in mind. Meanwhile the messenger was beholding the greatness of the army, and its good qualities, and the circumstances of the king and his prudent management, and the affairs of his Creator and His power, and the descending column of fire with its majesty, and he likewise saw the saint of God ant the terror which hedged him about, the like of which had never been beheld, or the like of it heard of in preceding ages. And when the children of Israil had celebrated the feast, the king gathered together his assembly, and had proclamation made throughout his army, and sent word to his chief commanders to assemble into their presence; but placed him in confinement in a certain place so that he might not witness their agitation or change of countenance. And when the leaders of the people were assembled, he read unto them the letter of the giants, and said to them: "Verily, never have I been overtaken by anything similar to this letter; and though I have waged wars for sixty years, yet never have I heard its like, nor anything approaching unto it." And when they heard the letter, their color changed and their heads hung down, and they said, "Never have we heard the like of this performance, nor have we ever encountered anything similar to it, or waged war with an army such as this is; but this war is one for God, and for us and for our children, and for thee, O king, overseer and master; and now manage us in accordance with the guidance and grace of God, and we will be obedient to thy supreme authority."

Then he brought out to them a reply which he had dictated, and he had dictated that which he had composed in accordance with the light of God- may His name be mighty- and he said to them: "This I lay before you as a reply that I have written, and as an address that I have drawn up, and if it seem to you to be the proper thing, I will send it; but if your opinion be that it should be abandoned, I will discard it."

CHAPTER XXIX.
AN ACCOUNT OF THE REPLY SENT TO THE GIANTS.

It began, saying:

"In the name of God, the Supreme King, the God of worlds, the Compassionate, the Merciful, the God of gods and the Lord of lords, the King of kings, the Knower of secrets, the One resolute in wars, the God of Ibrahim and Ishaq and Yaqub, the Destroyer of infidels, the Annihilator of tyrants, the Destroyer of the obstinate, the Extirpator of intriguers, the Collector of the dispersed, the Scatterer of the confederates, the One who brings the dead to life, the One who puts to death the living: His hand is above the highest of the highest, and under His outstretched arms is eternity, the heavens and the earth are in His grasp, the holy angels in all their numbers and the whole creation He did create by His omnipotent power, and the spheres and the heavenly bodies moved under His guardian care, their rapid course He stopped by His mere word, and put in motion moving bodies by His divine authority. Of this Lord do I ask assistance, and upon Him do I place my trust, and in Him do I grow strong, and Him do I fear, and His mercy is a shield unto me, and unto my children, and He is my sufficiency and excellent Protector.

But now to proceed to what follows: I am Yush'a, the son of Nun, the mortal and spiritual, the disciple of Kalimu'l-lah (Moses), a child of Khalilu'l-lah (Abraham); upon me and my people be peace, mercy and success. But as for you, O ye people of unbelief and false religion and profligacy and given over unto the curse, corrupters throughout the land, destroyers of the servants of God, worshippers of idols, who kneel down unto images, who bow down unto the celestial bodies, who are subservient unto spirits, who are slaves unto matter; let not the peace of God rest upon you or upon your people, and may He not make your way successful or your circumstances prosperous, and may he not have pity upon your young or feel compassion for your aged, may He make your condition ruinous and scatter your confederation; and this He will do by the terror of His power and the omnipotence of Hid will; for He is a hearer and answerer (of Prayer). Ye have mentioned (may God not let the remembrance of you remain, may He not make you successful in a single thing, may he not bring to completion anything which ye have begun, may He not leave any life unto you), that ye are reinforced, joyful with good news, irresistible in power, and fully with good news, irresistible in power, and fully able to undertake the expedition towards me, and engage in battle with me around the place on which I worship my Lord, which is the Mount of Blessings and the holy spot, even the house of our Lord and the place of our God. May ye have no life and may that not come to pass, and may ye not behold my place with your eyes, and may the hallowed plain not be polluted with your armaments, and may ye never boast that ye have trodden my soil, nor of even having approached unto my soil, nor of having got into my vicinity through any way whatever. But now as to your granting a delay; God does not grant unto you a delay in undertaking the journey until after the expiration of thirty days, and therefore I will not put off the journey unto you, nor will I grant you any delay except only for seven days, and then I will make the attack and with me will be the troops which I will select; and they who have been tyrannical will then find out with what overthrow they shall be overthrown. Therefore know for a certainty and consider and understand and be aware, that I shall bring on the battle between me and you in the place known as el-Qaimun, and it is verily the place in which ye shall not get away from me, nor depart from it, nor flee unto another place, but there destroyed by the slaughter of the sword and put to death by strangling and burned with fire and annihilated in vengeance; it shall not be unto you, O deluded ones, as ye now boast it shall. And I do not say as ye say, that they will march with me six hundred thousand men who did wage war with Greater Misr (Egypt), and did eat the sacrifices of the Passover, and around whom the angels kept guard, and who crossed the sea in dryness and journeyed through the wilderness without any guide, the pillar of fire sheltered them from the cold by night and the pillar of cloud sheltering them from the heat by day, and whose food was the manna from heaven during forty years, and for whose sake the bitter water became sweet, and for whose sake the water brought forth from the rock, and who heard the voice of the Creator- His mention be honored and His name glorious, and who beheld the quaking of the mountain at his command, and the destruction of Sihun and `Ug and their people, and who inhabited their cities, and for whose sake the water of the Urdun was stayed until they passed through it, and who fought with Yariha and with the cities which ye well know. I do not boast that there march with me giants, as ye boast; but there march with me twelve thousand young men, who entered Midyan in safety, fought with it and came out safely there from. There is with me no thunderbolt such as ye mention; but with me is the Lord of thunderbolts and the Controller of the blowing winds, yea with me is the One who takes away spirits and who hears the voices of prayer, the Creator of the whole creation and the Distributor of gifts, whose greatness is glorious; He is the God whose creation is all gods and whose servants all kings are --blessed be He and exalted, in His company are three angels of His of whom, one brought the water of the flood upon the world to destroy corrupt transgressors, and another scattered the king of Babil (Babel, Babylon) and his host, and demolished their fortress and changed their languages, and another lifted up his five fingers five kings of cities, even Sadum (Sodom) and its buildings and riches and animals and plants, and rained down upon it sulphur and fire and salt. He who has in His company thousands and myriads of thousands of angels similar unto these; what king then shall boast that he can stand before this King, whose rank and dignity is so great, whose position is so exalted, by whose mighty power the kings were destroyed and in obedience to whom the true believers believe? What army can stand before Him? What giant can march out against Him? What great commander can escape from Him? Unto what place can any flee from Him? Have ye not heard of our poems wherein we say: "There is no power or might except in God, the Exalted, the Great; if it (the power of God) came to the water, it (the water) stood still. The idols heard it and fell down one after another?" Know that ye are the ones are consumed, taken and killed: ye shall not find a place unto which to flee, nor a refuge on which ye may rely; ye are ruined, ye are discomfited, ye are destroyed, yea, your people and your men and yourselves, and ye have made your wives widows and have rendered your children orphans; ye have made your enemies to rejoice, and ye have cut off your purpose before its allotted season and have made weak your power before its time; ye were ungrateful with the Divine mercy, and God took it away from you; ye have been rebellious against the Divine compassion, and God has ceased to bestow it unto you. The earth was broad for you and not narrow for you, either in condition or riches, but now there is no place or locality for you; seeing ye have opposed the One to whom belongs the great and high dominion, and have become subservient unto a decaying image, and your intentions are bent upon the destruction of the holy, favorite people, who are the guardians of the children of the prophets of God, and of His apostles. Who did sware unto them by His Name- mighty and glorious- that He would apportion unto them this territory, and now this Lord- blessed be He and exalted- says unto His people, that He will guard them as a man guards his eye. O ones whose hearts God has obscured and whose understanding He has bewildered and whose spirits He has extinguished and the light of whose eyes He has darkened! Have ye not heard what happened through our friends unto your friends, when our ancestor Ibrahim, el-Khalil- peace be upon him- marched against your friends, and in his company there were only three hundred and eighteen men; yet he did destroy of them five kings, the like of which was never heard of, nor did their fight cease short of Dimashq (Damascus)? Have ye not heard what befell the people of Misr, and what signs and wonders God- may He be exalted- showed, because of their abusive revilings? Have ye not heard how my comrade did kill the Nil with his rod, and crush the sea by his prayer, and stop the water through the reverence and respect which he inspired, and turn back the Divine wrath by his intercession, and cause the Divine compassion to descend by his words, and put to rout armies with his hand, and how the earth swallowed up those who opposed him? Have ye not heard what happened unto us in the wilderness, and what befell Sihun and his kingdom, and `Ug and his pride, and Bila'am and his sorcery, and the kings of Midyan and their host, and the kings of esh-Sham and their pomp? Have ye not heard what happened unto us at the Urdun, and what happened unto us at the Urdun, and what happened unto us with the kings who joined in a confederation and assembled together to attack us? Have ye not heard how I called upon my Lord to prolong the day, and the day did return after its setting, and the day stood still for me like as if it had been a whole year? And it will thus stand still for me a second time during your destruction. I do not boast that I am a giant, or the disciple of a giant, or the child of a giant. I boast that I am the disciple of Kalimu'l-lah, the mortal and spiritual; and a child of Khalilu'l-lah, the foundation of the prophets and the top branch of the pious; I boast in the myriads of the holy who march around my army. I am no giant, but the Lord of the giants is with me; and yet my stature from the ground up is five royal cubits. I do not dress in armor even, and in coats of mail and helmets; but my clothing is tunics of dark blue and purple and variegated crimson, and the royal crown is on my head with the name of my Lord inscribed upon the crown. I ride upon a white colt whose saddle-cloth is of purple and its saddle of pure gold: these are my distinguishing characteristics and these are my boastings. Aided by the prophets, surrounded by the holy, the Lord of creation is my armament, and His angels my triumph, and His omnipotent power my reliance. And He is the beholder of your affairs as well as the affairs of me and my people. We believe in no lord but Him, and no king besides Him: and He is our sufficiency and excellent Protector.

CHAPTER XXX.
THE ACCOUNT OF WHAT HAPPENED BEFORE THE DEPARTURE OF THE MESSENGER FROM YUSH'A THE KING.

When the children of Israil heard this address and this reply, bowing down, they prostrated themselves before God, and spake, saying: "How adorable is He who has guided thee! How adorable is He who has enlightened thy heart! How adorable is He who was illuminated the light of thy intellect! How adorable is He who has ennobled they soul! How adorable is He who has sanctified thy spirit! How adorable is He who has ennobled thy soul! How adorable is He! Thou hast consoled our souls and hast strengthened our hearts; Thou has nerved our loins, Thou hast lifted up our heads, Thou hast exalted our renown, Thou hast spread abroad our glory, yea our friends do exalt, for Thou hast destroyed our enemies and hast annihilated their host. And now we are swift and zealous subjects in Thy presence, ready to go unto the horizon of the seas and to the abyss of darkness and unto the burnings of fire. And this is the approval and opinion we express to our master the king and let him carry it out by transmitting this letter; for in it lies the destruction of our enemies and their ruin, and the breaking up of their hearts and their purposes, through the power of God and his omnipotent might." And the king gave immediate direction that they should make known to him the list of the enumeration of those who had been chosen from the army, and that they make proclamation for them to mount at once. And scarce an hour passed before three hundred men had mounted, every one of whom was renowned fro manly qualities and skill, chosen men they were, the like of whom or better rank and file than theirs had ever been seen. And the officers returned and said unto him: "O our master and our lord, there have assembled for thee three hundred thousand chosen men, and if thou wert to command that there should be chosen as many more as they, we would be prompt to do the same, for in our lists there are other three hundred thousand men, but they are separated from us, and the mustering of them will be accomplished in the course of a week." And Yush'a the king answered them saying: "If He would destroy our enemies with six hundred thousand men, He is able to destroy them with three hundred thousand men." And he commanded that the messenger should be brought, for he knew that he was possessed of sagacity; and he-read the letter to the multitude in his presence. Thereupon he said unto him: "Look at and behold what I have collected unto me in one single hour, with regard to whom I do not need to bother myself about their provisions, or look after their condition, and in three days there will gather unto me a number equal to them, through the power of God and His omnipotent might; so now make known to thy companions what thou hast witnessed of the affairs of God- Mighty and Powerful- even the power of His people. And lo! I am about to march right on the tracks of my letter, with the help of God and his power and strength."

CHAPTER XXXI.
AN ACCOUNT OF THE RETURN OF THE MESSENGER, AND WHAT HE DID WHEN HE REACHED THEM (I.E. THE ENEMIES).

When the messenger had heard the king, and his speech, and the reading of the letter and its words, and perceived the discipline of the army and its staunch condition, he took the letter and immediately started out on his journey, with head down-cast and heart rent asunder and color changed and eyes weeping. And when he arrived at the army of the enemy, he found them assembled together in el-Qaimun. And when he beheld them he weep with great weeping and cried with a loud voice, and said to them: "O woe unto me for you, and sad am I for your sakes. Whither ye marching? Is it unto the sea of darkness? Unto him who does not listen to a word of yours, nor sends back peace to you? Unto those ye have no stability or durability or permanency; every affair of theirs is in earnest, no jesting or secret backbiting exists among them. Therefore give attention unto the reply to the letter, that ye may know that God is over all things, powerful, ere I explain unto you what I have witnessed, and inform you of what I have beheld; for if I should continue for one year explaining and expounding about Him, I should not make known His substance or make known any of His attributes."

CHAPTER XXXII.
THE ACCOUNT OF THE READING OF THE LETTER, AND WHAT THE ENEMY DID WHEN IT WAS READ.

He then took the letter and read it unto the company of the kings. Now the inscription written upon it was:

"To the company of reprobates, rebels, libertines, infidels: the calumniating, rebellious, polluted, and cowardly people; the filthy, self-disgraced, whose destruction is near at hand, and whose ruin is just impending:

"From the excellent, the faithful, the associates of purity, light, glory, firmness and victory, and possessed of authority and influence, the celebrated, far-famed, set-apart, chosen, protected by God, assisted unto victory by His power, sheltered under His mercy and compassion; and He is their sufficiency, and upon Him is their reliance."

Upon the reading of this inscription they wept until their eyes flowed blood, then they opned the letter, and a man read it in a plaintive voice, while they began beating their faces and wailing over themselves to greatest excess, until they had finished its reading. And the letter was not completed before their inwards were attenuated, and their heads bent down, and their hearts broken, and their tears poured out and their intellects bewildered; and they were neither able to arise from their places nor rest in quiet in them, for dementia and perturbation had seized them. Then they cried out while weeping, and said: "Woe unto us and unto our children, we have destroyed ourselves, we have brought about the violation of our women, we have waked up the sleeping lioness, we have stirred up the crouching lion, we have let loose the elephant that was tied, we have roused the bull that was tethered." And now their tongues jabbered on in their mouths, stuttering exceedingly as if tongue-tied, and they neither understood what they said, nor what was said to them; yea, they were deaf, they were dumfounded, they were stunned, they were bewildered, the hair on their heads stood on end and they tore their garments. Then there came unto them the sheikh of the magicians, and with him was the mother of Shaubak, the son of Hamam, who was skilled in magic and who worshipped the great luminary and the seven stars, and along with her was a crowd of the magicians and wizards and conjurers, and these calmed them, saying unto them: "O ye who turn back! Ye have wrecked your army before ye have seen the enemy, and ye have killed yourselves before your time; not thus should the leaders of the army do among the flock, ye have unnerved the men with fear, ye have slaughtered them without a sword being used. Sit ye down with us and listen with reason unto what we say, and bring hither the messenger whom ye sent, and consider what he shall describe unto you." So they brought the messenger, and he began to describe the king (Yush'a), and the feeling of awe that he carried away with him, and he described the army tribe by tribe, and the Divine ordinances which he had witnessed, and the grand condition of affairs which he had beheld. Then the messenger said to them: "O assembled men, accept my counsel, and do not yield yourselves unto any other; for I have seen what ye have not seen, therefore know what shall overtake you by surprise, for after three days will come the hasty rush and flight, and the abandonment of our baggage, and the saving of ourselves and our possessions; for, verily, he (Yush'a) is a magnificent commander, he is not to be held as contemptible and insignificant; and against this people neither sorcery nor stratagem is possible. Every god whom ye worship and serve will flee away from before their God whom they worship. Have ye not heard what happened unto our master and chief Bila'am?" Thereupon the band of magicians went apart by themselves and the mother of Shaubak with them, and they agreed in opinion that they would work out for them his (Yush'a) discomfiture, so as that he should not come unto them. And they commenced operations and built their altars and offered up their sacrifices, and they were answered in that which they requested, and they sat down in order that they night deliver their mandate with power and force. But God delayed this unto them, according as He willed. Blessed be He and exalted, for the consummation which He brought about.

CHAPTER XXXIII.
THE ACCOUNT OF THE SETTING OUT OF YUSH'A THE KING UPON HIS EXPEDITION.

When Yush'a the king desired to start out on the journey, he met with the saint of God, el-'Azar the imam- peace be upon him- and said unto him: "Go forth, invoke a blessing upon thy people and bless them, and when we have proceeded on our journey continue repeating it, and do not cease standing before thy Lord humbly beseeching Him, until thou hearest tidings of us." And el-`Azar, th imam, went forth to the tabernacle and blessed the people, and invoked a blessing upon them, and then he proceeded to bid farewell to the king, and to weep, while the priests invoked upon him safety and success and prosperity and good-fortune. Then he commanded the Liwanites to make proclamation throughout the army, in accordance with what our master Musa, the Prophet --the most excellent peace be upon Him,- had enjoined upon them in the Holy Law at the command of God, where he says: "When ye go out in battle against your enemies, and see horses and footmen, and a people more than ye, be not afraid of them; for God thy God is with thee, which brought thee up out of the land of Misr"- and so on to the end of the chapter. And this having been executed, at close of the proclamation, Finahas (Phinehas), the son of the imam- peace be upon him, his cousin sounded on the two trumpets of clamor, and the congregation of the children of Israil shouted with one voice, and the angels in heaven and on earth did tremble by reason of their shout. And having knelt and bowed down, they then mounted and journeyed forward until they arrived in the vicinity of el-Lejjun.

CHAPTER XXXIV.
THE ACCOUNT OF WHAT HAPPENED TO THE CHILDREN OF ISRAIL IN THIS PLACE.

When the children of Israil arrived at el-Lejjun, before they were aware of it, Yush'a and those who were with him had got inside of seven walls of iron, and the device of the magicians against them was consummated, in order that the decree of God- may He be exalted- might be accomplished, with regard to exalting the renown of Nabih, the king of the two and a half tribes, who was beyond the Urdun; for not a thing of this work had been effected, but for the sole purpose that the renown of Nabih might be glorified, and his name spread abroad. And one object of this was, that if the giants were put to rout they would cross over with them, and while they were fatigued, follow hard after them; and it was in their purpose so (to do). And another object of this was, to show up the result of the counsel of the deities of the giants; for Finahas alone did blow on the trumpet and dissolved every perplexing machination which the magicians had wrought. And another object of it was, that the embarrassment of king Yush'a might continue until the souls of the giants had become strong and their hearts elated and they settled down at ease; that the army of Nabih might cross over east; then would the magic from the west be dissolved, and the army issue forth and close upon the enemy from all directions, until not one of them should escape. Now this war was the last war that Yush'a the king witnessed; for the time of his death had drawn near. And we will recount what happened, so that even a hearer shall be as if he had been a witness of it; and he will be astonished at this great stratagem, and will praise Him who is powerful over all circumstances and spirits. Blessed and exalted and glorious be He above all that the ignorant heathen mention. Mighty be his name; and He it is from whom help is to be sought, and in whom trust is to be placed.

CHAPTER XXXV.
THE ACCOUNT OF HOW GOD FACILITATED THE ESCAPE OF THE CHILDREN OF ISRAIL FROM THE MAGICIANS.

When Yush'a beheld what had come to pass unto him, he remained in great perplexity and exceeding fear, and began to desire of his Lord that a dove might alight upon him from the doves of Nabih his cousin; and he had not finished expressing his desire before the dove alighted in the room, and he praised God- Mighty and Powerful: then he looked at it and knew that deliverance was certain. And he commenced and wrote a letter unto Nabih, his cousin, which I am about to make mention of, by the will of God and His assistance.

CHAPTER XXXVI.
A STATEMENT OF A COPY OF THE LETTER

"I WRITE onto thee, O my cousin- may God protect thee and take care of thee, while I am sad of heart, weak in strength, with weeping eyes, humbled in soul, on the very verge of destruction, and three hundred thousand men along with me; for the stratagem of the magicians has been accomplished upon us, and I and my people are imprisoned and perplexed inside seven walls of iron, and in front of us are thirty six kings in complete joy and universal exultation, while we are in sadness and weeping and fear thereby. And now such affair as this had not been effectuated against us, except only that there might be accomplished what God- may He be exalted- desires with reference to the exaltation of thy renown, and the spreading abroad of thy authority; and God, God is the One, I my cousin, Who makes weak and makes strong. And truly thou knowest what covenants and compacts exist between me and thee, so rise up immediately and do not sleep; and if thou art asleep, awake: and if thou art awake, run; for I and the company of thy brethren, who are looking for deliverance from God- exalted be He- and thee, are imprisoned inside seven walls of Iron at el-Lejjun, and the host of the enemies are in el-Qaimun: so let not slackness nor rest nor laziness nor hesitation overtake thee, but outstrip the blowing winds and make manifest that by which thou shalt be remembered unto the end of the gliding ages, by the will of God and His assistance." And when Yush'a had finished folding the letter, the dove did not wait until it had been tied on to its wings, but snatched it in its bill and flapped its wings and soared aloft.

CHAPTER XXXVII.
THE ACCOUNT OF NABIH AND WHAT HE DID.

Now Nabih was sitting upon his judgment throne, his waist girded up and on him a green robe and a green turban, and he was engaged in looking into the judicial affairs when the dove threw the note into the room, and he opened it and read it, and his eyes gushed forth with tears and he cried aloud, at which the court became agitated. And he himself then cried out at the top of his voice: "Assembly of my brothers and my cousins and my comrades! Follow me, and reach your brethren; for they are imprisoned by magic inside seven walls of iron at el-Lejjun. Assembly of Men! Haste! Haste!!" And they that were around him shouted out with a mighty shout, the sound of which was heard unto the horizon of heaven and to the regions of the earth, which were their assigned lands. And now the shout increased and voices were intermingled, and there mustered immediately, as though they had been for a long time and period prepared and equipt, six thousand men whose garments were white and their horses red, and six thousand men whose garments were red and their horses white, and six thousand men whose garments were green and their horses black and six thousand men whose garments were black and their horses piebald; not to mention the various colored and renowned ones who were many and without number. And the women and children joined in rendering aid. And there went forth of the men an innumerable multitude; and Nabih went forth, riding upon a celebrated colt that was spotted like a leopard and was fleet as the winds, and behind him was his army and he was saying: "Fire! Fire!! No rest and no repose! And the shout rode up on high, and a wonderful warning presented itself in the sky, so that the birds dropped down one after another and fled away from the great wind into the desert, and wild animals did not remain quiet in their dens, and from these was witnessed (an omen) the like of which had never been beheld in the past. And when Nabih drew near to the great meadow, he halted until his army had collected together. And it came to pass that the mother of Shaubak went up to a lookout she had in el-Qaumun to worship the great luminary according to her custom, and when she beheld the luminous star- that is to say Nabih- rising up out of the east, she made haste to descend unto her son, and she said to him: Lo! A luminous moon is rising up out of the east, and about him are brilliant stars- meaning Nabih and his soldiers; and if he be of our enemies, O woe unto thee and woe unto me; but if he be for our assistance, then it is well with thee and well with me." And he became enraged at her because she had hastened unto him with woe, and he killed her- may God have mercy on her. And he put on his armor and took his bow and arrows studded with pearls and corals and them made proclamation throughout his army and advanced alone against Nabih; and when he drew near him and beheld him, he said unto him: "O Nabih, what is the matter with thee that thou barkest?" And he answered him: "Yes, my name is Nabih, the son of Gil'ad the son of Makir the son of Manashsheh the son of Yusaf to whom was given the kingdom of Y'aqub the son of Ishaq the son of Ibrahim who killed the kings of esh-Sham; and my lord has sent me to anathematize thee and destroy thee, and as my father killed thy father so will his (my father's) son kill his (thy father's) son: and now, O thou anathematizes! O thou unclean one! Who art thou?" And he said to him: "I am Shaubak, the son of Hamam the son of Fut (Phut), the son of Ham, the son of Nuh whom God did bless at the time he came out of the ark. Stand for me until I shoot first, and then I next will receive (thy shoot)." And Nabih said unto him: "Of God I ask assistance, because thou shalt shoot first and kill first. Let drive, O anathematized, O, unclean one!" So he (Shaubak) let drive at him with the first arrow: now he was- God curse him- a man shooting with determination and confidence who never missed the mark. But Nabih dodged his head, and it passed by him and did not hit him. Thereupon he shot at him a second arrow; but Nabih lifted himself into the air, and it passed between him and his saddle. And he shot a third arrow; and he (Nabih) countered it with his right hand. And Shaubak the son of Hamam began to desire to flee away, and Nabih said unto him: "Whither dost thou flee, O anathematized, O unclean one? I have received from thee three witnesses (of thy skill), now receive of its kind one witness from me: take this from my right hand which God has blessed- and to Him belongs the mighty power." Then Nabih shot it, and the arrow rose up to heaven and reversing came down into the head of the man, and penetrated to his belly and to the belly of his horse, and penetrated to his belly and to the belly of his horse, and plunder into the earth to a depth of five royal cubits, which is twelve cubits according to this cubit, and in that place immediately a fountain gushed forth, which is called `Ain en-Nushshabeh (the Fountain of the Arrow) unto this time. And when the children of Israel witnessed this miracle, they shouted out in hinor of God- Glorious and Mighty- saying: "There is no power or might except in God." And when Yush'a and they who were imprisoned with him heard them, God made a revelation unto him, saying: "Speak unto the priests that they sound with the two trumpets." And when they had done so, the walls crumbled and fell down; and the army closed in upon the enemies, and the trumpets of the angels were heard from heaven. And Yush'a said to the day: "Stand still for me," and it stood still: and to the winds: "Assist me," and they assisted him. And while the enemies were hurling from the east, the west wind was returning each missile unto its hurler, and thus was it also from all quarters. And as to the man who had the thunderbolt with him, when he hurled it, it leaped back upon the enemies and killed of them one thousand men; and the sword continued doing its work among the rest of them, until. The horses plunged in blood up to their nostrils. Then said Yush'a to his people: "This day has annihilated the power of the confederates and of the allies of the confederates. All the children of Israil should offer praises and halleluiahs to the King of kings and Lord of lords, who has rescued them and preserved them, and protected them, and delivered them, and uprooted their enemies." And the king was offering praise, and saying: "God is the one who acts as the Hero for us in the wars, God is His name." And the children of Israil followed him, while all of them were saying: "Who is like unto Thee, perfect in holiness? O, One who dost inspire terror! O Revealer of secret things! O Doer of wonders! O One who dost protect His servants and those who love Him, in every place wherein they dwell!" Now, this is one of the paragraphs of our master Musa the Prophet- peace be upon him, in his hymn of praise at the sea. And Yush'a moreover said: "God shall fight for you, and ye shall hold your peace." And this also is one of the sayings of Musa the Prophet- peace be upon him. And they lodged on the field of battle and rested that night; and they ceased not to commemorate God the whole night long, with hymns of praise and halleluiahs, until the rising of the sun, secure from any attack, amid great noise and merriment and gladness and booty; now that their enemies were destroyed and the remembrance of them blotted out. And God is the Victor, the Protector, the Guardian, and He is our sufficiency and illustrious Protector.

CHAPTER XXXVIII.
AN ACCOUNT OF WHAT WAS DONE DURING THE DAYS OF DIVINE FAVOR.

Now the length of this period was two hundred and sixty years. And the well ordered arrangement of the days of Divine favor existed during the days of Jush'a the king, and after him until the termination of this period; as I am about to mention and set forth. And they (the children of Israil) continued keeping the Sabbaths and the solemn assemblies- I mean, the new moons and the feasts, and from the era of the king they continued giving the land rest, one year in every seven years; in this year there was neither sowing nor cultivation, but yet every one had what was needed. And the children of Israil were delivering over to the Liwanites the tenth of all that came to them, and they possessed of every seed-sowing and fruit, and animal and other things. And the Liwanite was delivering over the tenth of this unto the high priest. And the children of Israil had another tenth, which before God they were disposing of, for themselves and for the imams and the infirm. And when they planted in the ground a new plant, its fruit was not eaten, except when in the fourth year the imam ate it, and then in the fifth it became released and made free to everyone. And the Hebrew slave who had served seven years was emancipated, and dominion over him was taken away. And when an Israilite, driven by want, sold his child and himself, there was always to him a right of ransom, and his account was settled, with reference to his years of service to come, on a basis of wages. And if there was not found for the Hebrew slave either a near or distant relative who would ransom him, he was set free in the year of jubilee; and so like was it with their lands which had been sold. And there was in every seven years a division of the land among the tribes, with reference to overplus and deficiency. And they always had chiefs whose duty it was to write up the calendars and keep record of the things which were brought to the treasury. And the firstlings of animals and seeds and fruits were carried unto the minister; and not a single ram or sheep or ox was sacrificed except upon the altar on the Blessed Mount, unless it was defective and was of the seven species, such as, the deer and the roebuck and the buffalo and the gazelle and the antelope and the giraffe. And they had judges who gave decisions for them, as to the commands and prohibitions (to be observed) at all times, so that they might keep them with right observance. And no one of them was able to commit an abomination, such as infidelity and other things of magic. But that it was brought to light, and the doer of the shameful thing, before he was aware would be apprehended, even though he was in the most remote parts of the assigned lands, for this was revealed by the jewels which were on the minister. And this minister would make a woman drink of the water of the temple, when her husband had suspicions against her; and if she had indeed been unfaithful to him and had become defiled with some one else, he would curse her; for if she was innocent in this regard, then she would return unharmed; but is she was guilty she was detected and immediately destroyed. And likewise it was that, no one did kill an innocent person, but that his murderer was made known by circumstances which were brought about, and the truth came to light. And there were transgressions and shortcomings and brutal deeds which the slaves did without due consideration, these did the minister, the imam, assume upon himself on every fast day, which is the tenth day of the seventh month wherein expiation is made for souls and spirits, such as for the raising of leavened bread during the feast of unleavened bread. And there were orders of the Liwanites, some of them wrote the Law, and some of them wrote hymns of praise and the genealogies, and some of them watched over the treasury of the children of Israil; and some of them had charge over the constant, perpetual burnt offering, and the continual ceremony in the temple; and some of them had charge over the anointing ointment, and the aromatic incense, and the perfume of the sacrifice, and the flour and the oil, and the candlesticks; and some of them had charge over the vessels of the temple and their arrangement; and the duty of looking after their condition; and some of them selected the animals (for sacrifice) out from the doubtful ones; and some of them did the sacrificing; and some of them sprinkled the blood upon the altar; and others of them did place in position the victims; yea, every company was organized for its special official work, and did not leave what had been prescribed unto it. And the continual burnt offering was offered up before the rising of the sun and after the going down of the same; and at the time when the blood of the burnt-offering was shed upon the altar, the priests sounded the trumpet on the summit of the Blessed Mount, and then the imams sounded in every district, and it was but the wink of an eye before all the children of Israil knew that the sacrifices had been offered up on the altar, and they rode up to pray; and the prayer was accepted, and the blessings were simultaneously bestowed, and Grace was full and Mercy all embracing; yea, circumstances were well ordered, and affairs were known and understood through the Divine light and auspicious favor; for the union between them and their Lord was close. Now this is an epitome of the whole. And the children of Israil were continually, addressing and consulting God, who guides with His mercy. And He is our sufficiency and illustrious Protector.

CHAPTER XXXIX.
THE HISTORY OF THE DURATION OF THE DAYS OF DIVINE FAVOR, UP TO THE TIME OF THE BEGINNING OF ERROR.

YUSH'A the son of Nun, reigned forty-five years, and at the approach of his death, he assembled the children of Israil and put them under covenant and bound them to an obligation that they would carefully keep what the Prophet Musa- peace be upon him- did, when he bid farewell. And he selected twelve chiefs from the congregation of the nine and a half tribes, and when he had tested them as to their knowledge and aptitude for administration, he cast lots over them in the presence of the congregation of the children of Israil, at Merj el-Baha (Meadow of Beauty); and the lot of king fell upon a man whose name was Abil, the son of the brother of Kalab, of the Judaic tribe. And he invested him with the royal authority and jurisdiction, and placed on him the crown, and had proclamation made throughout the congregation that they should be obedient to his commands. And he commanded him to be obedient unto the minister of God, and allow him an inspection into all his circumstances, and not to carry out a matter before that he had made it known to him. And Yush'a, the son of Nun- peace be upon him, died, and they buried him in Kefr Ghueirah: and Kaleb his comrade died, and they buried him near him. And this new king entered upon administering the government of the people, and he walked with them in perfect ways. And the report of the death of Yush'a reached the king Mab, and he sent and collected troops, and advanced against his territory; and this king (Abil) mustered his people, and God assisted him to gain the victory over them, and awe of him fell upon the remainder of his enemies, and he conquered territories and added them unto the assigned lands. And he reigned nine years, and then he died. And after him, Tarfi'a of the tribe of Afrim (Ephraim) was appointed successor and, when he was invested with the kingship, the king of `Amman (Ammon) marched against him; but God assisted him to gain the victory over him, and he continued in rule during the period that God had decreed to him, and then he died. Thereupon after him, up to the end of the space of time, which has been previously mentioned- and it is two hundred and sixty years, there were nine kings appointed to the office, who succeeded one another from all the tribes, and continued in their ruling two hundred and fifteen years; for Yush'a the son of Nun had reigned for the rest of the years. And the last of them was Shamsham (Samson) the king, who was unique among them: no one was seen as handsome as he, and he obtained greater victories over his enemies. Yet nevertheless, strength, and beauty and success and perfection shall be adjudged unto those who follow after them in the footsteps of those who have preceded them, and who act in accordance with their deeds, and offer sacrifices similar to their sacrifices.

CHAPTER XL.
THE HISTORY OF THE VICEGERENTS OF THE LORD, AND OF THE MINISTERS OF THE DAYS OF DIVINE FAVOR, DURING THE PRECEDING PERIOD THAT HAS BEEN MENTIONED.

When the death of el-Azar, the imam- peace be upon him, -drew near, he did as Yush'a the son of Nun had done, and collected the leaders of the children of Israel, and put them under a covenant and bound them to an obligation of obedience, and bid them farewell, and then bid the temple farewell, and worshipped his Lord; and when he came walking out, the holy odors were fragrant on the borders of his garments. And having gone to Kefr Ghueirah, he stripped off the holy garments which were on him, and placed them upon his son Finhas- peace be upon him- and he died and was buried in Kefr Ghuweirah; and all the children of Israel wept for him, after the custom of their fathers. And after him his son was installed, and he did as his father had done. And when his death approached, he also bound them to a covenant, and offered up sacrifices, and bid farewell; and having gone to Kefr Ghuweirah, stripped off the holy garments which were on him, and put them upon one of his offspring who was to succeed him, and then he died and was buried in that place. And after him there were installed five ministers for the Lord, and they served Him with acceptable service, and did as they who had gone before them had done, even up to the period that has been mentioned; and its days were well managed, adorned with the Light and with celestial and terrestrial happiness, up to the installment of `Uzi, the last of the vicegerents of the Lord in the days of Divine favor, and he was a young man. And the king of that time died, and another king was not appointed. Now the number of the years of the earth, from the time of Adam up to this time, was three thousand and fifty-four years. And there was gathered unto them, before the death of Shasham, a great multitude, so that if it was spread over the earth it would have filled the world, by reason of the abundance with which God had blessed them, and multiplied their possessions. But now there came to pass that which Musa, the Prophet- peace be upon him,- had spoken of in the address that he delivered; "Y'aqub shall eat, and be satisfied; Israil shall wax fat;" and let it be looked up to the end of the chapter in that great song. For then they did go astray from the way which he had prescribed unto them, that they should keep to and do. And the Omnipotent is our sufficiency; the Most Glorious, the One who is slow to chastise the rebellious.

CHAPTER XLI.
THE HISTORY OF THE BEGINNING OF ERROR AFTER THE DEATH OF SHAMSHAM, THE KING OF THAT TIME.

Now he was the ruling judge over the children of Israil, and took great revenge upon the nations, and destroyed a multitude of them. And when they were informed of his death, they assembled and bound themselves together by oath, and great zeal took possession of them. And when they read in the books of Bila'am, that these people could never be destroyed except by unbelief and pollution, they began to have recourse to devices to obtain a knowledge of how to work magic, and they did not leave a place, however remote in distance, which was prescribed for this profession, but that they sent messengers in search of it; and they obtained there from an ample share of the appearance of miracles, the like of which dupe the common people. And they sent some of the learned doctors from among their companions, and with them this knowledge; and they arrived in the neighborhood of the house of God. Now there was at this time no king administering the government, nor saint overlooking the holy matters. And the doctors entered into dealings with a company of the children of Israil who were people of pride, and expounded unto them the secret doctrine, and instructed for them one hundred men of the people, and wrought it out through men of the people, and wrought it out through their agency. And they inaugurated this audacious procedure and action, on a hill to the south of the Blessed Mount, and the place, from the sum of their number, received the name el-Miat. Thereupon they set to building up the place and offering sacrifices to idols, which effect no profit either in the present or in the future. Then the company removed, through fear of the children of Israil, to the west of the Blessed Mount; and on their going, their like followed after them, and they settled in a village on the slope of a mountain, and the place, from the number of their company, received the name el-Miatai, and in it they resided a brief time. Thereupon they removed from it; for they had multiplied in numbers and increased and branched out, and the place, on account of their great number, received the name Fer'ata. And God did not manifest His rebuke nor anger, until the affair of these infidels had reached unto all the leaders of the children of Israil, throughout all their assigned lands. And when they became careless and negligent about rising up against them, and had turned aside and become polluted; for some of them were overcome with cowardice and laziness, and others of them were engrossed, each one in his own possessions and wealth and riches and pride, and supposed that poverty would not overtake him though he might over-ride the world; and others of them were jealous, and the greater part of their will was bent towards waywardness. And the saints of God were overcome with blindness and confusion and cowardice; for envy was rife in the tribe of Finhas, and discord reigned among them. Now when these infamous deeds and brutal affairs were carried out, the angels shrunk away from them, and the Creator became angry at them and took away His presence from them, and from the Blessed Mount; and the light which had shone forth in the temple departed, and the Divine fire which had not been separated from the offerings upon the two altars was taken away; and decline was perfected in them, and disaster came upon them; for their sight was blinded. And we take refuge in God from misfortune, and of Him- mighty be His name- do we ask assistance.

CHAPTER XLII.
THE ACCOUNT OF HOW THE BEGINNING OF ERROR WAS STOPPED AMONG THE PEOPLE.

When it was the mourning of the second day (of the week), the first (day) of the year 361 of the reign of Divine favor- which day is known for greatest calamity and mightiest disaster and long lasting sorrow and wide-spread grief, which is like unto the day on which our father Adam was expelled from the garden, even the day in which was announced his death and the death of his seed- `Ozi, the imam, the saint of God whose greatness was spoiled and whose glory was ruined and whose holiness was destroyed and whose light was extinguished, passed, in the mourning of this day- the calamities of which have been mentioned- to the temple, and lifted up the veil of the inner holy house, and he beheld none of the signs of Divine favor. And he looked, and lo! dense darkness, and a black cloud spread abroad within the house, and he remained performing alternate service during the third day and the fourth; and when it was the morning of the fifth day, he looked at this darkness, and lo! it had spread and enveloped the foundations of the house; and then he knew that God- Mighty and Powerful- had become angry at them, and had taken away the light of His omnipotence and mercy and compassion from the place and from the children of Israil. And he began to gather up the vestments of the temple and the vessels of gold and silver, which had been from the days of the Prophet- peace be upon him,- and went out from the tabernacle. And God revealed unto him, in the Blessed Mount an open cave, which no one had beheld in that place before that day, and he took all that he found in the temple and placed them in that cave. And when he came out of it he wrote upon its mouth an inscription in his own handwriting, and made a list of what he had placed in it, and distinguished it with signs; them he turned to look again, and could not find neither cave nor sign nor writing. Thereupon he lifted up his voice in weeping and wailing and lamentation, and there gathered unto him the company of the Liwanites, and the twelve chiefs who acted with him, and likewise the seventy wise men, and they made inquiry of him as to his weeping and crying, and he informed them of what had been revealed to him. And when he explained unto them and their people, they rent their garments and beat their faces and bowed down their heads, and assembled their company and began enumerating what things God- Mighty and Powerful- had bountifully bestowed upon them, and what they now beheld of punishment and banishment and sorrow and calamity, and they did say: "Woe unto us and to our children after us, and how great is the exultation of the enemies over our misfortune! How great is the joy of the confederates over thee, O Israil! thy guardian is taken away, and who will now look after thee? Thy prop is taken away, and who will now support thee? Thy king is taken away, and who will now help thee? Thy power is taken away, and who will now strengthen thee? The Compassionate has become angry at thee, and who will now show pity? Signs were shown for thy sake, Misr was devastated for thee, the Divine power appeared in thy behalf, the sea was divided that thou mightest cross, Fir'aum and his people perished that thou mightest be preserved, manna descended for thy sustenance, bitter water became sweet to satisfy thy thirst, the voice of the Creator was heard for thy instruction, the rock brought forth water to test thee, `Amlaq was put to route at thy desire, the Creator let the Divine power dwell round about thee for thy protection, and His name alighted upon thee that thy enemies might have fear of thee. He placed the pillar of cloud as a sign of His tender compassion for thee. He closed up the two mountains of the valley el-Mujib (Arnon), that thou mightest pass over safely. He destroyed Sihun and `Ug, that thou mightest inherit their cities and possessions. He struck with terror the kings of `Amman and Mab and Midyan, that thou mightest plunder their cattle. He stopped the water of the Urdun, that He might display thy power and make prominent thy glory and exalt thy fame. He killed the seven tyrant kings, that He might give to thee their land and their cities, and their kingdoms. He gave over to destruction those who assembled together for thy slaughter. He extirpated Shaubak the son of Hamam, and those kings who were assembled with him to slay thee. He commanded the heavens and the earth to guard thee and protect thee. He removed the calamities of the skies and stars from thee and from thy county. He surrounded thee with the greatest prosperity and the largest blessing. He assigned unto thee the most exalted places, and the most glorious of which is the Gate of Paradise. He gave unto thee a kingdom in which no one boasteth besides thyself. He bestowed abundantly upon thee His grace, the like of which was never heard of in former ages. He assisted thee with His angels, and His omnipotence. He enveloped thee with His mercy, and surrounded thee with His compassion. He took thee into His keeping with joy on His part, and took thee under His protection among his own. But thou hast forsaken His worship, and renounced belief in His name, which should be exalted, and thou hast worshipped one that has not the power to remove calamity even from himself. Ye have not regarded those who became infidel, and your Lord has disregarded you. Thou did'st cover up from him, and He covered up His face from you. Our master Musa, the Prophet- the most excellent, peace be upon him- led you aright, but ye did not believe him. He informed you, but ye hearkened not unto him. He instructed you, but ye obeyed him not. Yush'a, his disciple, made covenant with you, but ye sported with him. Whither does your flight tend? Whom will ye find refuge for yourselves? From whence will ye help for yourselves? Who will rescue you from your enemies? Ye supposed that your victory resulted from the multitude of men, when, lo, the victory was the result of good behavior. Where are those who know our leaders? Where is the one who has pity on our infants? Where is the one who hears our voices? Where is the one who makes atonement for our sins and transgressions? Where is the one who makes manifest our power? Where is the one who renders our glory conspicuous here?" And they now felt remorse where remorse profited them nothing, while their weeping became great and their lamentations violent. Thereupon they took vows upon themselves that they would commemorate this sorrow, on the second and fifth days (of the week) always, until the favor of God- glorious be His might- should return unto them. And He is the one who knows when it will return; and we pray Him to remove His anger, and let fall the veil of His protection over us, through His greatness and compassion. Lo, He is a hearer and answerer (of prayer).

CHAPTER XLIII.
THE HISTORY OF THE ERRING MAN WHO WAS ENVIOUS OF THE DESCENDANT OF FINHAS THE IMAM- PEACE BE UPON HIM.

Discord had arisen between the descendant of Finahas (`Ozi) and his cousin Ili (Eli), whose name being interpreted means; the insidious. This erring man was of the tribe of Itamar (Ithamar) the brother of el-Azar the imam. Now the right of administration belonged to the tribe of Finahas, and it was the one which was offering up the sacrifices upon the brazen altar, and stone altar. And this man- the insidious- was fifty years old, and being great in riches had obtained for himself the lordship over the treasure house of the children of Israel; and he had obtained, through the knowledge of magic, what he had acquired of riches, proud rank and wealth. And his self-importance being great in his own estimation, he gathered to himself a company, and said unto them: "I am one to whom to serve a boy is impossible, and I will not reconcile myself to this, and I hope that ye will not be content to have me do this." And the company answered him: "We are under thy command, and under obedience to thee: command us in whatsoever thou willest." And he put them under covenant that they would follow him unto the place where they purposed going on the mourning of the second day (of the week). And he offered up offering on the altar without salt, as if he was ignorant, and immediately started out on the journey with his outfit and company, and cattle, and every thing that he possessed, and settled in Seilun (Shiloh). And he gathered the children of Israel into a schismatical sect, and held correspondence with their leaders, and said unto them: "Whoever desires to behold miracles, let him come unto me." And there was collected to him a multitude in Seilun, and he built for himself a shrine there, and organized matters for himself in it on the model of the temple, and erected in it one altar, on which he might sacrifice and offer up offerings. And he had two sons, who used to gather the women into the temple in the mourning, and lie with them, and would eat up all that was present of the offerings of wine and other things. And this man continued diverting the people by magic, for the space of forty years; for God-exalted, exalted be He; glorious be His might- delayed this unto him. And there was Shamul (Samuel) of the tribe of Harun, the Liwanite, the magican and the infidel; for his father had delivered him over to him (Eli) when he was four years old, saying unto him: "This is a son whom I have received in fulfillment of a desire, and it occurred suddenly to my mind that this boy ought to serve in this temple throughout the days of his life." So the erring man received him, and instructed him, and revealed unto him hidden things; and he grew to be as potent in the working of magic as he himself was. And blessed be God who does not punish the rebellious, except after long delay and showing mercy unto them.

CHAPTER XLIV
THE ACCOUNT OF THE CAUSE OF THE DESTRUCTION OF THIS ERRING MAN, AND HIS SONS AND COMPANY.

When the nations heard of the schism among the children of Israil, there gathered together of them a multitude of those who were inhabiting Yufa (Joppa) and Ludd (Lod, Lydda) and Beit Jibril and Ghuzzeh (Gaza) and other places, and they carried out the plan of making an attack upon the company that was in Seilun. And the army of the erring man went forth to meet them, but it was overthrown and put to rout, and there were killed of his companions four thousand men. And the troops returned to their friends, and said unto him (Eli): "Forsooth the cause of our route is, that the ark of gold was not with us;" so he delivered unto them the ark, and sent forth his two sons with them, and the flower of his army, in place of the first (army). Now they of the nations who had assembled had arranged an ambush, and upon the salling forth of his army, the army of the nations closed in upon them, and the sword did its work among them; and the ark was taken, and the two sons were slain. And one of those that had escaped safe, stained his garments with their blood, and came to their father, while he was sitting upon his seat, and said to him: "Disastrous news for thee; for thy two sons are killed, and my garments are even stained with their blood, and the ark of gold has been taken, and the sword has annihilated thy people." And when he heard tidings such as this, he threw himself backwards off his seat, and his neck was broken and he died. And when his daughter-in-law heard of this calamity- now she was big with child- the pains of childbirth grew violent in her, and she died. And so this man received reward for his action in this world, and he shall also be brought to account in the next. Blessed be He, Whom no affair escapes, and from nothing is hidden. Blessed be He and exalted.

CHAPTER XLV.
THE HISTORY OF BOKHTONASSUR (NEBUCHADNEZZAR), THE KING OF EL-MAUSIL (MOSUL), WHICH IS FOUND IN THE BOOKS OF THE CHRONICLES OF HIS DEEDS.

He was one of the kings of the Persians, who had conquered the countries and subdued the people, and the kings obeyed him. And he restored the authority od all the kings of esh-Sham, and they went to the king of el-Quds (Jerusalem), and entered into agreement with him that they would come under the rule of Bokhtonassar, and become submissive to his decrees. And they continued so twelve years; but when it was the thirteenth year, they broke the compact and revolted, and he pardoned them. And when he warned them, and they were not affected with fear, he marched against them in the fourteenth year, and destroyed whomsoever of them he met. And he directed his march toward el-Quds, and besieged it till he captured it, and he killed in it with great slaughter, and took its king and put out his eyes and sent him to Beit-A.., and burned all the buildings and the edifice which Sulaiman (Solomon) the son of Dawid (David) had constructed. Then he turned aside towards our country- that is this country- and made proclamation therein, that: "Whosoever was found remaining in it after seven days, the shedding of his blood would be permissible." Thereupon he took to goading the people and driving them out unto every country, and brought people from el-Furs (Persia) and settled them in this country, the home of the children of Israil, who now got to the most remote parts of the world, scattered and dispersed throughout the regions east and west. And the word of the Holy Law came true: "And God shall scatter thee among all people, from the one end of the earth even unto the other end of the earth." And after a certain time had passed by, letters were brought back from Persians who were dwelling in their (the children of Israil's) territory in esh-Sham, regarding the earth's refusing her crops and fruits; for when the fruit promised well the destroying blight would waste it. And the letters in regard to this reached the king, and he had the leaders of the children of Israil brought before him, and made inquiry of them about this state of affairs, and they said: "The cause of this is our removal, and the abandonment in it of the service of our Lord; and we do praise God for its disorder, so that we may return unto it and serve our Lord upon the Holy Mount, and offer up offerings as He commanded us in His Book, by the hand of His Prophet--peace be upon him." And the king replied to them: "Go and build the house of thy Lord and offer up the offerings, and serve your Lord as was your custom, and I will assist you." And they said to him: "Give unto us a writing by thy own hand unto all our brethren, who are scattered abroad throughout all the regions; for we cannot return except we all go together." And the king gave them a writing of his hand, permitting them to journey to esh-Sham. And they departed from his presence, glad and rejoicing for what God had kindly bestowed upon them. And the imam and the king sent letters to every place, saying: "Know that the king- may God make him powerful- has granted us permission to go up to the holy place and build it up, and offer up the offerings upon it with the service that is acceptable. And now it is necessary that ye make haste, you and your harem and your children and all that ye posses, that we may assemble and go, and carry out the orders which he has commanded unto us, concerning the service of our Lord- Mighty and Powerful." And the people all came together, and the offspring of Yehudah (Judah) said to them: "We will unite all of us and go to el-Quds, and build it up, and we will be one word and one soul." But the offspring of Harun (Aaron) and Yusaf (Joseph) said to them: "No, but, on the contrary, we will go up to the Mount of Blessing, and build up the holy place, and we will be one soul and one word." And they persisted in the dispute, until it became necessary that they should come together into the presence of the king. And he decided in favor of them (the descendents of Aaron and Joseph) after this manner: the children of Israil, the friends of the Blessed Mount, assembled with the book of Musa, the Prophet- peace be upon him- and relied upon what it is said in designating the Blessed Mount, and no place else, as the proper place; and the offspring of Yehudah assembled, relying upon what certain books written after the days of Musa, the Prophet- peace be upon him- designated with reference to Beit el-Muqadda (Jerusalem) being the place. And the books were brought and read in the presence of the king; and when he had carefully considered this matter, he saw that the intention of all was the Blessed Mount. But Zorobabil (Zerubbabel) answered and said unto him: "O king, the book which I have furnishes me with arguments in favor of Beit el-Muqaddas, and the offering up of offerings therein; wouldst thou then compel me to go up and offer up offerings upon the Blessed Mount?" And Sanballat the Liwanite answered him, saying unto the king: "The books which Zorobabil has are a lie and a fraud. Permit me to throw them into the fire; and this, my book, if he is able, let him take it and throw it." And the king gave permission unto Sanballat to throw the books of Zorobabil into the fire, and he did this, and they were burned up. Thereupon he gave permission unto Zorobabil to throw the book of Sanballat, and he took it, and said: "My books are mine alone, but the Holy Book belongs both to him and to me." And the king answered, saying unto Zorobabil: "I see that thy books are false; why didst thou abstain from throwing his book?" Thereupon, he (Zorobabil) feared lest he be put to death, and he took the Law and cast it into the fire; and it jumped out of it. And he asked permission of him to throw it in a second time; and it was not affected by the fire in the least. Thereupon, he humbled himself before the king, beseeching him that he might throw the book a third time; and he granted him permission, and he took it and spat upon a paragraph, and cast it into the fire, and the place which had been spit upon burned, and then it sprang out into the bosom of the king. And the king immediately became angry at the children of Yehudah, and put to death immediately of them thirty-six souls of those who were present. But Sanballat, he and his company, obtained great honor with the king; for the king gave him gifts and presents and chain necklaces and bracelets, and invested him with the silk robe of honor, and promoted their leaders, and sent them away with the whole multitude of Israil who returned from the first exile, and their number was three hundred thousand men. And thereupon they followed the true religion, after having been unbelieving; and pursed right guidance, after having wandered into error. And God accepted them and broke the chains of their captivity, through the mercy He had for them and the compassion He felt, and the remembrance He had for the covenant with Ibrahim and Ishaq and Y'aqub- peace be upon them. And the king sent unto all the Persians who had taken up residence in their assigned land, and removed them from it to their own country; and the people (of Israil) entered into their assigned land, which is their holy place. And they made the sacred apparatus similar unto that which was in the (former) temple, and they offered up a multitude of offerings; and the earth gave forth its good things, and returned unto its former beauty and splendor; and with the carrying out of this act (on God's part) nothing was withheld from them, nor did he veil to them what of Divine power He was wont to veil to their ancestors. And to every circumstance there is a cause, and to every fate there is a final limit. And of God do we ask assistance, because of what He has benevolently bestowed through His mercy, and upon Him be the trust put.

CHAPTER XLVI.
THE HISTORY OF EL-ISKANDAR (ALEXANDER THE GBEAT.)

The whole number of the years from Adam up to the time of king el-Iskandar was three thousand nine hundred and thirty years. And when el-Iskandar undertook the war against Dirawas (Darius) the Persian, he saw in his sleep an angel descending from heaven in the form of an imam, and clad in his robes, who said unto him : " Fear not, O hero, thou shalt conquer Persia ; for I am about to deliver him (Darius) into thy hand : behold God is with thee." So he (Alexander) attacked him (Darius) and killed him. And when each nation was subdued, its imams were brought unto him, in the hope that he might see one like unto that form; but he saw none. And when he came to Sur (Tyre) to conquer it, there were dwelling in its neighborhood some of the Samfii-at (Samaritans), and these el-Iskandar summoned that he might win them over to his side; but they would not consent, for they had bound themselves by an oath to this people. And he blamed them, and directed his march towards the region of Nabulus; and its people came out to meet him, and, when he beheld the form of the chief imam, he hastily descended from his animal, and prostrated himself before him. And when his attendants saw what he did, they also hastily- dismounted and prostrated themselves, while all the retinue wondered why he had been bent upon their destruction; and his companions said to him: "Verily, these people have bewitched thee." But he said to them: "They have exercised no power; by God, I am not bewitched, but only seized with great emotion; for, verily, at the time of my going forth against Dirawas there met me a man similar to this individual and like unto him in form, who said to me: Go forth against Dirawas, and fear not; for, lo, thou shalt kill him,' and thus it did come to pass." And el-Iskandar was moved with love for the Samat (Samaritans), and acted kindly toward them, and said unto them: " Verily, your God is the God of Gods and Lord of Lords." And el-Iskandar conquered all the country of el-Hind (India) and Faris (Persia) and er-Rum (Greece) and other places. Then an impulse led him to desire to see the whole earth, whereupon it was planned for him to make a journey into the land of Shades, upon she-asses which had colts, and he carried it out. And when they had tied the colts in the light, they entered upon a journey of three days into the darkness. Thereupon they took of the dust which was upon the ground, and then came out and examined it when they were in the light, and they found that the dust which they had with them was rubies and pearls, whereupon he regretted that he had not taken more of it than he had; for who would not take what someone has abandoned? And he said to his companions and his wise men: " In how much time, forsooth, can I see rapidly and quickly all the regions of the world? " And his wise men and companions said unto him: If thou desirest to see the world in one moment and in the briefest space of time, summon the skilled carpenters and command them to construct a car with screws and apparatus, which will with rapidity ascend and descend, then take four of thy trained eagles and tie them to the four corners of the car, and hang meat to the top part of the car, so as that the eagles cannot reach it ; for if the eagles crave the meat, they will ascend towards it, and the car will then be borne aloft through the air, until it be lifted up on high, and thou shalt see the buildings and what is round about them. And when thou hast the desire, the screws shall be put in rapid motion, and thou shalt have the meat changed about and hung below, and the eagles will go downwards in a desire to get at it and will descend with the car to the earth unto the level spot which thou desirest." And el-Iskandar did so and ascended into the air until he had seen the earth; then the eagles reversed and descended with him, until he alighted on the spot which el-Iskandar built up and called its name el-Iskandariyeh (Alexandria). Thereupon he came to the Mount of Blessing and acknowledged it to be the noblest of places, and the grandest: in praise to God — Mighty and Powerful. Then he proceeded to invest his companions with the authority over the territories, until he had gone over all the earth. And when his companions beheld his liberality to the children of Israel and his compassion upon them, and that he did not rebuke them for anything, whether it was a grave affair or a trifling action, they became envious of them; and his companions said to him: " Why does this nation transgress every religious ordinance, in neglecting to comply with the established statute? Why dost thou not summon it, and make instant demand of them concerning the establishment of idols and images? " And so he, at this time, commanded the imam — I mean the chief imam — and the chiefs of the children of Israel that, they should set up to him in all their habitations statues and images; and then said to them: " I am about to go unto Misr, and upon my return let me find what I have commanded. Then el-Iskandar set out on his journey. And the chief imam assembled all the leaders of the children of Israel, and they went up to the Mount of Blessing and fasted and prayed and offered praise, and humiliated themselves unto God — Mighty and Powerful — and He disclosed to them an excellent idea, to wit, that they should name their boys with the name of the king el-Iskandar. And they sent unto every place, ordering them to name every boy that should be born unto them with the name of the king el-Iskandar; and they did this. And when three years had passed the king el-Iskandar returned and came up from Misr, and when he came to the lands of the children of Israel, he saw in them neither statue nor image, and he reprobated this, and summoned the leaders of the people and demanded of them the reason. And they replied that they established unto him images, who were endowed with rational speech and moved like paragons of obedience and were quick to obey. Thereupon they brought forward immediately their children, of whom there had been gathered unto them a great number; and he said unto them: " What are your names?" And they said: "We are servants of the king el-Iskandar, who are named with his name." And the king and his disciples were pleased and approved of what they had done. And when the imam saw the satisfaction of the king in what had happened, he threw aside his restraint and said to him: " The reason of our neglecting the setting-up of idols is fear of our Lord — Mighty and Powerful — who has prohibited us from doing this, and when He — exalted be His fame and mighty be His name — saw the purity of the purpose, lie made known unto us that we should substitute our children in place of idols. And the king approved of this on their part, and said unto them, " I know that your God is the God of gods and Lord of lords." Thereupon the king bestowed upon them gifts and spread abroad the praise of their deed.

And unto God be praise and thanksgiving for His kindness, of Whom we ask mercy and pardon.

CHAPTER XLVIL
THE HISTORY OF ADRINUS (HADRIAN), AND HOW HE DESTROYED BL-QUDS (JERUSALEM), AND WHAT HAPPENED TO HIM WITH AFRIM (EPHRAIM) and MANASHSHIH (MANASSBH).

When this king, whose name was Adrinus, came to reign after el-Iskandar, he went down to Misr and killed a multitude of the Nasara (Christians) of those who believed in the Masth (Messiah); and when he had built a city in el-Hajar, he went down and besieged Beit el-Muqaddas. Now, prior to this, there was a city there called Yusaf and in it were two brothers, Afrim and Manashshih, who were Samaritans. And a certain Jew had gone up with some young doves, desiring to enter with them and make an offering in Beit el-Muqaddas for his sins; and he passed the night in Yusaf, and the two brothers took the pair of young doves and slew them, and substituted in their place two big mice. And the man arose in the night and went unto the priest who was installed in the temple and said to him: "Offer up for me this pair of young birds." And when the priest opened the basket the cheat of the two mice was discovered, and he laid hold of the man to kill him; but he said: "A trick has been played upon it. I passed the night at a lodging place in Yilsaf, and there were none there except two Samaritan lads, and I took up my journey in the night, out of my fear lest the offering which I was to offer for my sins might escape from me, and I knew not that this trick had been perpetrated upon it." And they sent unto the innkeeper, and arrested the two brothers to punish them; and when they con-
fessed that they had done this, they gave orders that they should be put to death', but certain of them said: " If we kill them their services are lost, rather let them be among the servants of the temple serving all their life long, eating

the thorn which is the food of birds and drinking water, and sleeping upon the ground." And after this Adrinus came down to Beit el-Muqaddas and besieged it; but the Jews used to go out of the tunnels which Solomon the son of David had constructed (one of which led) to Riha (Jericho) and another to Ludd (Lydda), and (the inhabitants of these towns) were giving unto them whatsoever they could eat and furnishing them with everything. And they (the inhabitants of Jerusalem) would go up on top of the walls and say to them (the besiegers): " See what our Lord does for us. He sends down upon us food; as He was wont to do with us in the wilderness, thus now again does He do." And they used to throw to them from above the wall fruit, both fresh and dried, and other things, and would say to them: Eat such as our Lord sends down upon us." And they would also say: 'Take unto you of what we have sacrifices to the king; for behold our Lord, as much as we are in need of, the same He sends down upon us; as He has wont to do with us in the wilderness, thus does He with us now." And Adrinus had given credence to them, in as much as the war had become fatiguing, and did reckon their statements to be true. Now when this affair came to pass, the two brothers Afrim and Manashshih came together, and wrote a note and worked it up in clay and threw it from above the wall to Adrinus the king, and it reached the king and he opened it and read it, and there was written in it this: "Do not deem their statements to be true; and if thou desirest that we should inform thee how thou mayest conquer the country — well and good; but, verily in consideration for that which shall enable thee to be victorious in the war, save our souls from death. Now if thou dost desire to get possession of the country, send unto Riha and unto Ludd and seize the mouths of the tunnels, and let not anything enter into them nor anyone go into them; and also seize Beit Lahm (Bethlehem), and demolish the duct through which there comes in unto them oil and water and sesame-oil and honey," And the king did according to what they said unto him, and he also sent and had brought into his presence the Samaritans Afrim and Manashshih, and they were present with him in besieging Beit el-Muqaddas. And he reduced them (the inhabitants of Jerusalem) to such sore straits, that women ate their daughters and men their sons. And he rose in attack against them while they were observing the requirements of the law, and when they beheld themselves spoiled of everything they sued for protection. And when they (the Romans) took possession, Adrinus gave orders that they should not molest the temple until he went in, and when he entered he took the priest who belonged to the temple, and said to him: "For whose name was this dwelling built?" The priest said unto him: "It was built for the name of the Creator of creatures." And when he had entered into the place, he beheld a painted picture and by its side an idol, and when he saw them he said to the priest: "This place was built for the name of the Creator of creatures and is this done in it?" And he seized hold of him to punish him; but he (the priest) informed him that it was a deceit which the Jews who served the idol had made, notwithstanding Harun (Aaron) had commanded that they should worship the Creator of creatures. And this wicked king saved Afrim and Manashshth from being killed; and Adrianus set up in the city an image upon a pillar in accordance with the will of Afrim and Manashshth, for the purpose of showing unto them (the inhabitants of the city) his rank, and it is there unto this day; and he also erected two images, and named the first image after the name of Afrim, and the second image after the name of Manashshth; and he gave orders to the leaders of the Jews that no one should pass by in front of them, but only behind them; and they are obliged to do this even unto this day. And Adrfniis went out from there unto Qiryat el-'Arba' (Kirjath-Arba) — which is Habrun (Hebron), and did like as he had done in Beit el-Muqaddas. And Manashshih said unto Adrianus: "Make in my name a bell, and let the bell be rung for my name." And he did so. And he went forth from there to Nabulus; for he desired to destroy it, but while he was in Merj el-Baha, and was elated upon his passing through it, they (the companions of the king) said: " If this is carried out, it (the Samaritan nation) will instigate a heroic revolt, and whoever sees this in Nabulus will be inflamed with the zeal of a hero." So they collected together and said unto him: " As far as it is possible unto thee, spare (the place)." And God moved his heart to pity, and he dealt kindly with it, and with those who led the troops in Nabulus; and he built there a town on Mount Gertzin, and called it Saqarus, after the name of his father. And the doors that were on Beit el-Muqaddas were of yellow brass, plated with silver and ornamented with gold, which Solomon had made, the like of which no one, though strong of hand, could ever make, and he (Hadrian) carried these away and placed them on the door of the dome which he had built on the ridge of the mountain that is over against Nabulus. And after this Adrinus went to Rumiyat (Rome), and the Samaritans came together and purified the places wherein Adrianus had been; and the Jews plotted a wicked thought against them, and went unto the king, and said to him: " Behold how thou art aiding the Samaritans and yet they are wishing thy destruction; make investigation and see how they have burned with fire every place wherein thou wast." And when Adrinus heard their words, he said: "We will kill every circumcised one." And he pronounced judgment of death upon the villages and upon every city, and prohibited baptism, and interdicted (the observance of) the Sabbath and feasts, wishing to ruin Nabulus and destroy it, like a field laid waste. And when the Samaritans heard of this mighty-calamity, they fled away, and were stricken with terror and hid themselves from the presence of this great wrath, and they did not enter into a house nor reside under a roof, and there remained for them no shelter except the deserts and forests and caves. And he came and burned the houses and crucified the teachers (of the people) and put to death its judges, and they did die in prisons by starvation, and their dead bodies were thrown out and not buried, and rights were infringed both as to themselves and their dead bodies, and they were persecuted in castles and on the roads. And when he came to destroy Nabulus, he began from the city gate on the west until he arrived at the four pillars that were above the declivity at the base of the mountain. And they captured there a man who was fleeing that he might not be killed, and he fled into the presence of Adrinus and conjured him, and said unto him: " I beg of thee, by the honor of the One whom thou dost worship, O king of the age, hear of me one word, and after that do with this nation what thou wishest." And when he had bound himself by oath he listened to him, and the captive said: " Send and make investigation into the conduct of the Samaritans, for though they do burn every place wherein a foreigner has been that they may purify it from his tracks, yet we have not done this out of malignity or hostility to thee. And the Jews have spoken unto thee only deceitful", because that we did render aid to thee in reducing them to straitened circumstances, and also because we did at once furnish thee with provisions." So he (Adrinus) said that he would no longer put to death anyone, and he showed favor to the city and did not destroy it. And he set up three images after his likeness, in the city on top of pillars, on the spot where the man fled away from being killed, and also two images on the aqueduct. And after this Adrinus died — may God have no mercy upon him — and he died in woe and every kind of affliction, and his reign had lasted twenty-one years — may God crush his bones. And the space of time from Adam up to his death was four thousand five hundred and thirteen years and seven months. And in those days the Book of Choice Selections was taken away, which had been in their hands since the days of Divine favor; and there was also taken away the Songs and Praises which they were accustomed to utter over the offerings, each offering according to its merits; and also the Hymns which they were wont to sing in the days of Divine favor: now all these constituted a library which had been preserved with greatest care generation after generation through the time of the prophets unto that day, by the hands of the chief imams. And there was also taken away the Book of the Imams which they had, wherein their genealogy was traced back to Finahas; and there was also destroyed the Annals wherein was recorded their birthdays and the years of their lives, and of these not one ancient book or chronicle was found, except the Law and a book containing their lives. But we have written up the years of the life of the chief imam, and a genealogy from the chief imam Aqbun; and this comes (in the next chapter).

CHAPTER XLVIII.
THE HISTORY OF AQBUN THE IMAM.

Now it was once said to him: " Brother of the king I everything in thy house belongs unto the king," and Aqbun said: The whole of it belongs unto God, and I have given over my spirit unto God and I will not renounce my Lord." And they (the Romans?) went and seized two men of the children of the imams, and said unto them: " Seek refuge in our gods, and ye can depart to your houses unharmed." But they utterly refused, and said: " We will not do that" so they killed them in punishment and threw their corpses outside the wall — that is the wall of Sebustieh; and they crucified of the wise men of Israel a company of thirty-six men on the gate of Nabulus. In that day the instruction of Israel was like as dust; there was no imam among them, nor wisdom, nor teaching of the Law, nor was any one able in the days of these kings to give instruction in the Pentateuch; except one in a thousand and two in a myriad. And the children of Israel continued in this calamitous state until Bab& Rabba arose. In those days 'Aqbun knew his wife, and she conceived and gave birth to a son, and he named him Natanal (Nathaniel), and this Natanal was the father of Baba Rabba who broke the brazen bird which was on the Mount preventing them from ascending it; for this the Romans and (their) magicians had done. After this the chief imam 'Aqbun died; but before he died he said at this time to his son Natanal: "O my child, be not troubled with regard to these times, or these calamities, or the power of the enemies; know that in a short time these distresses will disappear, for these calamities are tests sent by God upon us, that He may prove whether we ourselves are faithful and are not forsaking the worship of God our God. O my child, these calamities and straits will vanish away; for God — may He be exalted — is able to cause them to disappear from us." And the imam Aqbun proceeded to make a revelation unto his son in accord with this, and invoked blessing on him, and said unto him: " O my child, be on thy guard against worshipping another than God; for wert thou to be crushed under stones, God would give the strength to worship Him. And God will raise up from the one who will get the ascendancy over this infidel oppressing nation." And the prayer of the Rabbis Aqbun was granted at that time, with regard to all that he invoked for his son; for there arose from his son, Baba Rabba, and he brought about that which happened to the Romans. And at that the imam Aqbun died and was removed to his people: may God benefit us with his blessings. And all Israel mourned for him and wept for him thirty days.

CHAPTER XLIX.
THE HISTORY OF WHAT HAPPENED UNTO NATANAL FROM THE ROMANS, AFTER THE DEATH OF HIS FATHER.

When the Rabbis 'Aqbun died and was trans-
lated to his people, Natanal took the office of imam in place of his father.
And he knew his wife, and she conceived and gave birth to children, and he
was granted of her three children; his first born was Baba Rabba, his second
was Aqbun, and the third after these two was Finahas. Now when the imam
Natanal was granted his first born, he was for some time perplexed with
regard to him, as to how he should circumcise him; for the Romans at that
time forcibly prevented them from performing circumcision, and set over
them curators, that they might not circumcise their children, and there was
stationed at the door of the residence of the imam Natanal a deputy of the
king, named Jarman the Roman.

And when the Rabbis was granted this child, he took it on the day of
circumcision, and placed it in a basket and put wool on top of it and under
it, and said unto the maidservant that was with him: "Take this boy and go in
advance of us unto the field to the cave, and we will follow after and overtake
thee, that we may circumcise him; but let no one know what thou hast. Take
him and go out from the door of the house, while we will go out from the
rear of the house." And the maid took it and went out; and when she issued
forth from the door of the house, Jarman the deputy said to her: " Perform,
girl, what thou hast in mind, and fear not." And the maid went to the infant
to the cave and repeated unto the Rabbis Natanal the speech of Jarman; and
he in fear said: "The affair is God's." And they circumcised the little one,
and the maid-servant returned with it just as it was; and when she came to the
door, Jarman said unto her: " Rear him in peace, O my child." And when she
had passed, she repeated to the Rabbis the speech of Jarman, and he was
smitten with great fear, and said: "Who has informed Jarman of our business?
I cannot mollify his anger except with great riches. And the Rabbis was
worried, and went forth to Jarman, the deputy over his house, with his hands
full of gold. And Jarman said unto the Rabbis: "I will have nothing to do with
this, except only I will take of this just three dinars, so that thou mayest not
say that I am laying a plot for thee; for, verily, I will not make this known
unto the king." And when Jarman had bound himself by oath unto the
Rabbis, his heart became good, and the Rabbis made it to be remembered of
Jarman; and it came to pass that whenever they circumcised any of their
children in a cave, they would invoke a blessing on Jarman, saying in the
Roman language : " May God be merciful unto Jarman the Roman priest; "
and unto this our day, they invoke a blessing on him, immediately after every
circumcision. And the Romans did mix hogs' lard in everything that was eaten

and drunken, so that they (the Samaritans) might be afflicted with bodily infirmity. And the houses of prayer that we had were shut up, and they prevented us from going up on to the Mount, by means of a talisman which they fixed above it. And we continued in this strait and great calamity for the space of twenty years; until God comforted us, and saved us from the power of the infidels, and this was brought about by the hand of Baba Rabba.

CHAPTER L.
THE HISTORY OF BABA RABBA, AND WHAT HAPPENED TO HIM WITH THE ROMANS.

When the kingdom passed away from the children of Israel, and the Romans ruled, they gave over to judgment and crushed under the stones of torture many of the Samaritans, until they should abjure their faith and bow down unto idols; and many of the Samaritans perished through this cause. And the Romans suffered not one of the Samaritans to circumcise his child, but stationed trustworthy men of the Romans over the houses of the Samaritans to prevent them from performing circumcision. And the Samaritans were wont at that time, when a child was born unto them, to place it in a basket and cover it with wool and go with it to the cave and circumcise it under ground by the light of candles. And also, they the Romans prevented the Samaritans from ascending the Mount; for they said: " Whosoever goes up on to this Mount shall be put to death ". And the Romans placed upon the summit of the Mount a talisman, and this was a brazen bird, and it used to turn round with the sun howsoever it revolved, and it was so that if a Samaritan did go up, the bird would screech out: Hehraeus and they would know then that there was a Samaritan on the Mount, and would issue forth against him and kill him. And the children of Israel continued in this distress, until Baba Rabba arose; and in him there was a spirit of resolution and zealous patriotism. And Baba Rabba assembled the Israelitish community, and said: " How long shall this polluted nation go on dominating over you? Arise, let us lift up the children of Israel from this oppression, and let us be zealous for God — may He be exalted, as our father Finahas was zealous, and there remains to him a goodly remembrance unto the end of the ages. And now know that I have resolved upon the destruction of the Romans, and I will purify Mount Gertztm of them but not a thing can be accomplished for us, except by the destruction of this bird which is stationed over the temple, and this cannot be effected for us except by a stratagem which God has revealed unto me. Now ye know that this is a time of infidelity, and they have many kings, and my plan is to send Lawi, the son of my brother, to Qustuniyeh(Constantinople) the city of the Romans, that they may learn what they talk about what it is that makes them powerful, and may gain a knowledge of their religious sects. And he shall go in the garb of a Christian monk (or) priest, and no one will know him, and the Romans will not know who he is; and he will come back to Mount Gerizim, and will go up to the church and make use of a stratagem to smash the bird; and when they (the Roman guards) attempt to repel him he will employ stratagem and get the giver to ascend the Mount, and will supplicate up upon it, and He will then give us the victory over our enemies ". And all the people said: "O our master, do what seemeth good in thy sight." And he said: " Give unto me your own handwritings, that after his coming back your souls will stand by him." And they did this And Baba Rabba led forth the son of his brother to Beitil (Bethel) in the presence of the people, and said unto him: " Be attentive however thou mayest be, and set thy mind upon learning everything, and be on thy guard that thou cease not to read the Pentateuch night and day, and God shall help thee in all thy doings." And he sent away Lawi, the son of his brother; and he pursued his journey seeking Qustuniyeh. Now Lawi was an intelligent, knowing, acute and pure man, yea, in him was found every virtue; and he arrived at Qustuniyeh, and sought after learning and diligently applied himself, and he obtained what he sought for; and with his keenness of intellect he continued reading for the space of two years, and there remained no one among all the Romans more learned than he. And he arose to such eminence in learning that the Romans used repeatedly to come to do him reverence, and by reason of his eloquent attainments in learning they made him Archbishop, and he was elevated to the highest rank among them, until kings used to come to his door, and no king could assume the kingly authority without his orders, nor put on a crown except by his command. And it came to pass at the end of thirteen years that he said unto the king: " I have a desire to visit the church which is on the Mountain of Nabulus". And the whole army assembled, and the king and the legions marched in his